W9-BPN-275

Globalising Education

This highly topical book charts how the tools of technology are altering the ways in which higher education is being delivered and received. It looks at the huge impact of the World Wide Web on current educational practice and what this means for the students and teachers involved. It also covers the other new technologies that support the delivery of what is now truly global education.

Divided into three clear sections, *Globalising Education* adopts a systematic and thoroughly researched approach to this exciting topic. The three sections examine:

- how global education is actually delivered in practice
- case studies which investigate current developments and applications in the USA, Europe, the UK and Australia
- conclusions drawn from the general issues covered, as well as an overview of what is happening now and what we might expect to happen in the future

This book looks at current developments in detail. It is essential reading for all those involved in education – whether as teacher, student or interested onlooker.

Robin Mason is Head of the Centre for Information Technology in Education at the Open University, Milton Keynes.

Routledge studies in distance education
General Editors: Desmond Keegan and Alan Tait

Globalising Education

Trends and applications

Robin Mason

London and New York

First published 1998
by Routledge
11 New Fetter Lane, London EC4P 4EE

Simultaneously published in the USA and Canada
by Routledge
29 West 35th Street, New York, NY 10001

Routledge is an imprint of the Taylor & Francis Group

Reprinted 1999

© 1998 Robin Mason

Typeset in Times by Routledge
Printed and bound in Great Britain by Biddles Ltd,
Guildford and King's Lynn

All rights reserved. No part of this book may be reprinted or
reproduced or utilised in any form or by any electronic,
mechanical, or other means, now known or hereafter
invented, including photocopying and recording, or in any
information storage or retrieval system, without permission in
writing from the publishers.

British Library Cataloguing in Publication Data
A catalogue record for this book is available from the British Library

Library of Congress Cataloguing in Publication Data
Mason, Robin.
Globalising education: trends and applications / Robin Mason.
(Routledge studies in distance education)
Includes bibliographical references and index.
1. International education. 2. Distance education. I. Title.
II. Series.
LC1090.M36   1998   98–14125
370.116-dc21   CIP

ISBN 0–415–18687–0 (hbk)
ISBN 0–415–18688–9 (pbk)

Contents

Illustrations

Table

Figures

Preface

Is the advent of global education a threat or a promise? This was the guiding question which informed my research for this book. My simple answer, having finished the book – though not the research! – is that it is neither. At the risk of putting off potential readers, let me acknowledge straight away that I find no evidence for the emergence of one or even several global players preparing to take over higher education on a global scale. Unlike the soft drinks market, education is unlikely to be dominated by a few giant providers. Why? Because it is too difficult; there is too little money to be made, too many complex issues to handle, and too great a need for 'people skills' rather than technical skills.

Can we all go back to business-as-usual then? I think not. The higher education market is changing rapidly and there is much evidence to support the rumours of large scale closures of existing institutions, of very different working conditions for staff at those educational establishments which remain, and of wholesale re-thinking of the organisational, pedagogical and technological delivery of higher education. Many of these changes are caused by or informed by the growth of some forms of global education. What my research shows is the increasing differentiation of the education market around the world, and hence the scrambling for position in that global market by existing as well as new education providers. Institutions which will survive the changes must be putting in place a strategy now – even if that strategy is to remain a community or regional organisation. While the number of global education providers will increase, the need for local institutions will continue in my view, although probably not at current levels.

What about the promise side of the equation? Is global education a movement to be welcomed? I find that the 'early adopters' of globalising trends in education are frequently enthusiastic about the benefits of global education for students, for educators and for institutions. I do not doubt these benefits, and have tried to describe them fairly in the book. However, as is well known, early adopters do not a mass market make. In my researches I met committed, enthusiastic and caring teachers and learners. What is promising for them, may not be so benign when applied on a mass scale, when less committed people and more unscrupulous organisations jump on to the global bandwagon.

The big issue in global education is the cultural one, and as I demonstrate throughout the book, most practitioners have hardly begun to tackle it. Much of the promise of the globalisation movement in education depends on how successfully cultural differences are addressed, once the first wave of enthusiasts give way to the mass adopters.

In developed countries, the financial squeeze on higher education, coupled with a wide range of technological and social changes, have already provoked great concern about standards of education and the quality of the learning environment (although perhaps there has always been such concern in the face of any kind of change). The growth of global courses is usually regarded as yet another unfortunate development which brings serious cultural problems to the already troubled waters of higher education. I have tried to show in the book the reasons why global education could actually be the solution, not the problem.

I have referred on many occasions throughout this book to specific Web sites: I have quoted from Web materials, and referenced urls for the reader to find further information. Obviously many of these will soon be incorrect, out-of-date or unavailable. Many of the programmes and even institutions I refer to will also change, perhaps before the book is actually published. This is a hazard I have had to learn to live with in my field! I hope the reader will be able to look beyond the detail and regard this as an attempt to document the first steps in the process of the globalisation of education.

Many people have contributed to my understanding of the complex issues surrounding the growth of global education. I wish to acknowledge the co-operation of all those who agreed to be interviewed for this research, and especially the staff and institutions figuring in my five case studies: Fuqua School of Business (Duke University), the Distance Education Centre (University of Southern Queensland), Jones Education Company, and IBM Global Campus. To my own institution, the UK Open University, I owe the most: several research visits were funded by the Institute of Educational Technology, but this affordance was a small contribution when compared to the many opportunities it has provided me for teaching, researching and thinking on a global scale.

Robin Mason
Institute of Educational Technology
The Open University
Milton Keynes

Part I

Issues in globalising education

In this first section of the book, I examine what I consider to be the major issues arising from the growing practice of global education. Taken together, these chapters reflect my research findings derived from the literature, from my own experience of teaching globally, and most importantly from Web searches.

The Web is a curious source of information for the researcher, certainly in the field of global education. There is so much posturing and positioning on Web sites, that without personal follow-through (and the best form of this is actually going to visit the physical site of the education provider), it is impossible to distinguish between vision and reality. Sometimes really significant practice is hidden away in the very back pages of an unremarkable Web site, whereas the opposite is more commonly found, namely, very insignificant practice is presented as a major undertaking. I was not able to investigate thoroughly every site to which I refer, and the reader may consider that on occasion I have been duped by 'Web promise'.

I have resisted pressure to provide a glossary of technical terms, as I firmly believe these are not useful vehicles for learning about technology. To those who disagree, I refer you to any of several Web sites which provide detailed and regularly updated glossaries. I have tried to use terms in a context which explains the meaning, whereas a precise definition often obscures the meaning.

1   The globalisation of education

Do we need it?

The reaction of many people to the notion of global education is resigned exasperation, querying whether we really need yet another revolution in the teaching/learning paradigm. The spectre of people dotted in continents here and there around the world studying the same Physics 101 course does not conjure up the image of a high quality learning environment comparable to the cosy picture of student-led seminars, heads bent over books in library carrels, passionate arguments in late night coffee houses, and brilliant lecturers spellbinding young undergraduates. Why is global education then such a burgeoning phenomenon? Are we being driven to this by non-educational pressures, or are we expanding in this direction because it offers educational benefits? And who is it that is leading the pack?

I begin by considering the extent of the phenomenon – how much education on an international scale is actually taking place? It is hard to avoid encountering the avowedly evangelical predictions about the educational implications of the digital 'this' and the electronic 'that', and the triumphalist announcements of the optimists introducing the education superhighway here and the virtual university there. It would be easy to think that global education is already established practice, with courses, programmes and whole institutions jostling for position in the global marketplace. Whilst competition amongst tertiary education providers is certainly brisk in most developed countries, the market in question, even for those offering distance education courses, is primarily regional, in some instances national, but not often international. In fact, the number of truly global courses, let alone programmes or institutions, is still very limited. Nevertheless, I can only conclude from my studies that global education is a phenomenon to be reckoned with for all those in higher education and training. My reasons for this assertion will unfold throughout the book.

The arguments for global education

There are a good many economic, socio-political and technological reasons underpinning current developments both of the plans for and the practice of global education. Perhaps they will prove to be the strongest forces driving change. However, committed teachers and educationalists would prefer to feel that a pedagogical rationale for a global student body or a global curriculum is the primary consideration. Undoubtedly there is a case to be made for global courses on purely educational grounds, and I have divided these according to the reach of the course, the access to the course and the development of the course.

The strongest argument relates to the benefits of a global student body:

> The diversity of participants made for a far richer course than I could ever teach myself. Take, for example, the time our correspondent in Istanbul reported on a lecture given there on medieval Christian philosophy by a Franciscan priest to the faculty of the (Islamic) University of the Bosporus. Well and good, the faculty opined when it was over, but it's too bad Christianity is not a truly rational religion, like Islam. Leaving aside the question of comparative rationality of religions, I think it is undoubtedly good for my students at Pennsylvania [University], taking a course on a very traditional, 'Western' figure, to be reminded that the whole picture looks quite differently if you happen to be in a different seat.
>
> (O'Donnell, 1996, p. 113)

Here is the case of a course on the work and thought of Augustine, taught face-to-face to undergraduates and beginning graduates on a traditional campus, being offered over the Internet in order to supplement the intake on such a specialised topic. Over 550 subscribers from around the world – Bangkok to Istanbul – joined up and undergraduates, scholars, and Internet-surfers all contributed to the discussions. The taste of global interaction given to this teacher by his first venture on to the information superhighway, left him concluding: 'I cannot imagine ever passing a semester in the classroom again without the umbilical cord to the network to energize, diversify, and deepen what we do' (*op. cit.*, p. 114).

O'Donnell's experience is echoed by many others who have discovered the educational benefits of a global student body. What is particularly welcome in this example is that the globalisation of the course mitigated against the usually dominant Western world view.

The second most compelling educational justification for globalised education is that of access. Whether potential students be geographically remote, time constrained, financially constrained, house-bound, disabled, or simply unable to find a course on the subject they want locally, there exist large un-met educational needs which every research report, policy study and educational analysis shows are increasing.

For an institution which has an access remit in its mission statement, global education is now part of the moral high ground and new technologies are providing them with the means for reaching out to people anywhere, any time, who want to learn. The UK Open University (UKOU) is one of the most prominent examples of an institution enshrining access to educational opportunity and openness to students of all backgrounds, not only into its name and mission statements, but into the very heart of the organisation: its preparation of course materials, its enrolment procedures, its tutorial support provisions and its commitment to helping similar, developing organisations around the world. This is how the UKOU rationalises the extension of this approach into a global strategy:

> The University is committed to addressing educational disadvantage and widening educational opportunities for an increasingly large and diverse number of learners. Its mission statement, with its emphasis on openness to people, places, and methods, underlines the University's commitment to respond to need and demand wherever the means of delivery exist. In the past, limitations of educational technology and funding have confined that ability to deliver to fairly strict geographic limits. Those constraints are rapidly diminishing. The OU now has the potential to extend educational opportunities to a much wider body of learners not only in the UK but throughout Europe and more widely in the world. In doing so, it has the ability more fully to satisfy its mission. It has the power to transform people's lives, without regard to geographic frontiers.
>
> (Open University, 1995)

Related to the notion of access is the third purely educational rationale for global courses: that the expertise of the few can be made available to the many, such that those in remote areas can have the same access to educational resources, specialist courses and renowned experts as those located in large cities and developed parts of the world. A student who signed on to a Web-based course on the Principles of Protein Structure offered by Birkbeck College, London listed one of the main advantages of this virtual course as the easy and informal contact it provided with a large number of fellow scientists around the world. 'Everyone is on first name terms and the mailing lists, along with the group structure, provide a convenient way to discuss issues raised by the course material, and to deal with any problems people may be having' (OLS News, 1995).

Athena University, one of the newly established electronic universities, sees its mission as providing high quality educational opportunities on the Internet as inexpensively as possible. It is able to carry out this mission by utilising the Internet resources of the entire globe (http://www.athena.edu).

The expertise located at one university in the USA is shared with ninety students in three other countries: Mexico, Finland, and Estonia, providing access to a Certificate Programme in Distance Education, through a combination of audioconferencing, computer conferencing and recorded media (Collins and Berge, 1996).

Finally, and some might say most importantly, a good many areas of the curriculum are inherently global in nature and some particularly lend themselves to course development on an international scale, providing students with a much broader perspective than a course presented by a single lecturer or developed by a single institution. A good example of transnational course development is that of the European Association of Distance Teaching Universities which has encouraged the joint authoring amongst its members of two programmes: the European MBA and a comprehensive course in the humanities, entitled 'What is Europe?'. The advantage of this kind of international collaboration is elaborated by Trindade, President of the Portuguese Open University:

> In Europe, the very old universities tend to perpetuate rigid (not to say extremely conservative) educational systems. . . . This weight of tradition is reflected in university programs that have scarcely varied in format or designation for at least half a century, despite intense basic and applied research activity in advanced or innovative fields. . . . Distance Teaching Universities seem to be more accepting of new ideas or new models, more pragmatic in their approach to co-operating with each other, and more daring in their attitude towards transnational collaboration.
>
> (Trindade, 1996, pp. 40–1)

These, then, are the major advantages to global education as cited by some of the practitioners teaching and learning at the coal face. At its most visionary, the ideal of global education is one of a movement away from the bounded classroom, seen as a haven from the world, self-contained and static, to a dynamic synergy of teachers, computer-mediated instructional devices, and students collaborating to create a window on the world. Interaction with learners on a global scale leads to an increased awareness of the extraordinary complexity of interrelations and a relativistic comprehension and tolerance of diverse approaches to understanding.

Other advocates of the movement in this direction, however, see a range of less idealistic factors driving education on to the superhighway.

Pressures encouraging global education

The reasons behind the, in some cases, drastic reduction in funding of public universities, as well as the falling population of traditional 18–20-year-old students, at least in Western countries, are outside the scope of this book. Suffice it to say that financial pressure on institutions of higher education worldwide is probably the most critical factor forcing administrators and policy makers to look to global markets as a way of making up for falling government revenues and falling numbers of traditional learners.

While the search for new sources of revenue has provided the impetus for universities to look for new markets, larger social changes have steered that search towards globalisation. In fact, global education is a reflection or extension of society's increasing understanding of the interrelatedness and interdependence of the physical world. The development of this global consciousness has been heightened by the spread of global communication systems and particularly the entertainment media. 'Distance open learning appears to be uniquely suited to the emerging world order. As borders open up across the globe to traffic of almost every kind, so distance open learning flows increasingly across national frontiers' (Field, 1995).

Field contends that transnational education represents both an outcome of and a primary factor in the intensification of global interconnectedness. Education, he points out, used to be regarded as an essential element in nation-building. As with other social and political trends, education is increasingly being thought of as a commodity to be shaped according to consumer demand.

Some commentators on globalisation see the trend towards student-as-consumer as having positive educational outcomes. Teachers and course developers are being forced to consider the requirements of learners, and the global telecommunication systems allow students' opinions to be embedded into the learning environment.

> Technologically-mediated knowledge provides the basis for individual-ising learning in a more complete and active way. . . . Here distance is subservient to the discourse of open learning and 'educative' processes are displaced and reconstituted as relationships between producers and consumers in which knowledge is exchanged on the basis of the useful-ness it has to the consumer. It is therefore a discourse of open learning which might be said to more fully govern the practices of those operating at a distance in the postmodern moment, as increased marketisation is introduced into the provision of learning opportunities and mass markets fragment and become more volatile across the globe.
>
> (Edwards, 1995)

For Edwards, the globalisation of education through the use of telecommunications technologies will empower the learner and force the providers of education to concern themselves with students' needs, rather than with the transmission of a pre-established canon of knowledge. Educators, just like businesses, will have to become more flexible – in their staffing ratios, in their approach to students, and in their considerations of the curriculum. Various structural rigidities of traditional universities will have to be overcome: constraints on what constitutes the academic year, on where credits can be accumulated, and on how courses can be modularised. The kinds of courses which the global consumer is demanding are flexible, adaptable, portable and interactive.

Dangers of global education

Although the enthusiasts for the globalisation of education are more prominent in the media, they are probably equalled in number by the voices crying for a halt to the headlong expansion of global education on the superhighway. I have found it useful to classify their arguments as primarily cognitive, educational, social and cultural.

The cognitive argument is based on the fact that the new delivery mechanisms for most global education are electronic and rely largely on the digitisation and computerisation of knowledge. Many people decry the cognitive effects of learning from screen-based information rather than traditional text-based material, pointing to the breakdown of linear, narrative structures associated with the book, and the resulting fragmentation and superficiality induced by the hyperlinked structures of the Web and multimedia CD-ROMs. One of the more eloquent apologists for the culture of books is Sven Birkerts, who tots up the cognitive losses we are incurring with the rise of an electronic culture:

> In the loss column are (a) a fragmented sense of time and a loss of the so-called duration experience, that depth phenomenon we associate with reverie; (b) a reduced attention span and a general impatience with sustained inquiry; (c) a shattered faith in institutions and in the explanatory narratives that formerly gave shape to subjective experience; (d) a divorce from the past, from a vital sense of history as a cumulative or organic process; (e) an estrangement from geographic place and community; and (f) an absence of any strong vision of a personal or collective future.
>
> (Birkerts, 1994, p. 27)

Birkerts acknowledges that these are enormous generalisations, but he feels that they accurately reflect the comments of his students about their own experience.

The educational argument against global education centres on the undesirable aspects of consumerism, wherein learning ceases to be about analysis, discussion and examination, and becomes a product to be bought and sold, to be packaged, advertised and marketed. In the previous section I presented the case in favour of competition in course provision. However, just as there are many who do not accept its value in a whole range of social services, so there are those who view the growing competitive, consumer spirit amongst educators as detrimental to the learning outcomes (see, for example, Moore, 1996). This marketplace philosophy of higher education is particularly associated with distance education, which in turn is the foundation of the movement towards globalisation.

One example of the shoddiness of global competition in education is the number of MBAs offered by a range of Western institutions in the advanced countries of the Pacific Rim. Some are outright cons; others are just poor quality; many are 'sold' for high prices which are then used to defray the deficit incurred by students taught face-to-face in the home institution. Together with legitimate, high quality, well supported programmes, they all jostle in the marketplace to the bewilderment of prospective students, who have fewer standards for, and less experience with, assessing the quality of global courses than they have in judging local programmes.

Social arguments against globalisation are related to the breakdown of community. This phenomenon is part of a much larger, more complex web of changes associated with postmodern society; nevertheless, education, which has always been a net contributor to the positive benefits of physical communities, is now seen as undermining still further the physical experience of community and offering instead a much less substantial substitute in the form of virtual communities.

The global classroom does have a communal atmosphere: it has interaction between students and teachers, and networking and serendipitous encounters with other learners, both those following the same course and those simply out browsing, searching or talking on the Internet. There is evidence of many of the elements of traditional communities: people help each other (by forwarding information to each other which they think will be of interest; they answer queries from strangers, providing them with the benefits of their expertise, for no personal gain; they trade confidences and intimacies; they play games together; they meet regularly). Nevertheless, some observers of this new phenomenon see great danger and significant social loss in the demise of physical community and its replacement by virtual community no matter how educational:

> There seems to be a great difficulty in holding onto the truth – as obvious as it is – that ease and flexibility of switching do not constitute ease and depth in making human contact. Certainly the connectivity makes communication 'easier', but it achieves this precisely by rendering *contact* more incidental, more shallow.
>
> I suspect that every major technical advance in communication since the invention of writing has marked the path away from community rather than toward it. Community is, in the first instance, something to be salvaged from information technology, not furthered by it.
>
> (Talbott, 1995, p. 74)

Others warn about the loss of our fundamental assumptions regarding identity and subjective meaning by moving from the physical and substantial to the virtual and electronic. The notion of community has always been rooted in a sense of the particular and this has characterised our experience over millennia. The essence of our education system has been the community of the classroom and the physical reality of the textbook. It has changed relatively little over the past few hundred years.

> What we will have in the next few years is an education system that is part of computer culture. It is not just the physical environment that will be transformed. Whereas books have encouraged us to think in terms of a

> stable body of knowledge, a form of content that we can read, digest, learn, and know, computers dispose us to think differently – to be engaged in a constantly changing process where information is not stable or fixed.
>
> (Spender, 1995, p. xxiii)

The effects of this de-stabilisation on social and personal assumptions has been analysed at length by Poster (1990), who describes the dispersal of identity through computer networking.

Finally, the cultural arguments against global education systems are equally compelling, and hearken back, of course, to old concerns about imperialist attitudes, the loss of indigenous cultures and the relentless imposition of Western values. Global educators are seen as the new colonisers, insensitively spreading their own views of the world on to developing nations in the mistaken belief that they are actually helping people:

> The access to this sort of provision can be seen to have considerable educational (and possibly, social and economic) benefits to a developing nation. However, as an invasion, it can be seen to weaken national initiatives to develop local educational provision which might be better suited to local needs. It also creates the potential for a post-colonial dependency on another 'developed' nation.
>
> (Evans, 1995)

Evans argues that despite the value of global education in offering diversity of choice, this comes at the expense of encouraging local initiatives which value local culture and promote national beliefs, skills and knowledge. The potential power of globalised teaching to spread dominant ideologies and to crush emerging structures, whether wittingly or unwittingly, is the main cause for concern. Moore, who also expresses concern about the cultural implications of global education, says that truly international distance education courses would involve all participants (including the teachers, experts and Western students) in a re-examination of their educational philosophies, their views of the subject being taught and their cultural perspective of the content of the course. In practice, he feels, Westerners tend to be arrogantly uncritical of the assumptions underlying their teaching and unreflective of their fitness for teaching across cultures (Moore, 1996, p. 189).

Current practice

I have presented some of the most significant views of the enthusiasts and practitioners of global education and have outlined the wider pressures leading to the global expansion of higher education. I have also laid out the arguments of those concerned with the negative impact of global education. So having briefly considered *why* it is happening, and *why* some oppose it, I turn now to an analysis of *what* is happening under the guise of global education.

I suggested earlier that there is a good deal less global education being practised than would be imagined from reading newspaper articles, browsing the Web or listening to media hype. Let me begin with a listing of the various elements which I think characterise global education. Many self-designated global courses are in progress which do not meet all of these criteria; indeed, I have not found a single institution which could truly be said to be offering global education according to the following criteria:

1   students in more than two continents of the world able to communicate with each other and with the teacher;
2   an express aim on the part of the teacher or institution to attract international participation;
3   course content devised specifically for transnational participation;
4   support structures – both institutional and technological – to tutor and administer to a global student body;
5   operations on a scale of more than one programme and more than one curriculum area, with more than 100 students.

I have decided not to consider the various global initiatives operating at the level of primary and secondary education. While some of the issues I discuss will also apply to some extent to these schemes – cultural benefits and threats, cognitive effects of computerisation and screen-based learning, educational value of a global curriculum – I want to focus primarily on the higher education sector (including training and professional updating), and on the notion of a university without place, rather than on a classroom without walls.

Second, I know that there have been a number of global programmes running for some time, even quite large scale operations, which are based on print and postal systems only. I will not focus on these non-telecommunications-based programmes within the compass of my discussions because I consider that they have been effectively superseded by the advent of the Internet and global telecommunications systems. In fact, many of these programmes are already beginning to introduce elements of telecommunications into their support or administrative procedures (for example, the Centre National d' Enseignement à Distance in France).

As is apparent from some of my arguments so far, I will include current debates surrounding virtual universities and online courses, whether or not they are actually operating globally. I consider the issues and outcomes of these practices fundamental to the future of global education; indeed they are the forerunners of it.

Using the five attributes of global education listed above, I can discuss current practice on a continuum from courses with global aspirations to those already in operation.

A global student body

By far the largest number of 'pseudo-global' courses – and most originate from North America – have no face-to-face requirements, and all course material, administration and support are provided either electronically or by post. The majority of students are North Americans, but occasionally students abroad (British or Australian perhaps) will hear of the course and ask to enrol, particularly in specialist areas where a similar offering is not available locally. More commonly, a number of North Americans move abroad or are sent by their company during the period of the course or programme, and they continue their studies from the new country. These courses are global in fact but not in spirit – the content has not been altered; the interactions are amongst people of the same culture; the institution has not been re-engineered for a global mission.

Nevertheless, there are some courses and even programmes currently taking place which have students from a number of different countries and cultural backgrounds. For example, many training programmes offered by global companies have trainees in North America, Europe, Asia and Africa following the same course. The delivery medium of many of these training programmes is usually satellite television with the employees accessing from the workplace. In education, the delivery medium is usually the Web, and these courses and sometimes whole programmes, are now attracting a truly global student body.

An international aim

A most interesting class of courses are those where the instructor, often a single enthusiast within the institution, designs and writes a course (usually Web-based) and makes it available globally to anyone with access. In many respects this 'early adopter' class of courses provides the model of best practice for true globalisation. The big difference, obviously, is that these courses are free, are not accredited and are usually 'one-off'. Because of their outstanding success, the instigators move on to institutionalising (accrediting, charging, marketing) them. One example has already been mentioned: the Principles of Protein Structures at Birkbeck (http://www.cryst.bbk.ac.uk /PPS /index.html). Others in this category continue to be offered in their original form: for example, Roadmap is a free, twenty-seven lesson Internet training course which 80,000 people in seventy-seven countries had taken by email in 1994, and by 1995 the number had increased to 500,000. Spectrum Virtual University offers free courses about the Web and the Internet, as well as 'focus groups' for 'hands-on' learning in small exploratory teams (http://www.vu. org).

A few courses specifically aimed at a global audience, which nevertheless are fee-paying, accredited and on-going, do exist, and many more are in the planning stages. I have chosen two to present in case studies: the Graduate

Certificate in Open and Distance Learning by the University of Southern Queensland (Chapter 7), and the UKOU's Masters Degree in the same subject (Chapter 10).

A multicultural course content

There have for many years been twinning projects between universities in which one (usually a Western) institution develops a course or programme in conjunction with one or several (usually non-Western) institutions. Recently, the courses resulting from these collaborations have been delivered electronically. The Télé-université in Quebec has carried out this kind of course development with other French-speaking nations (Umbriaco and Paquette, 1996) for example, and many universities have long-standing arrangements with institutions in South America, Asia and Africa.

A number of franchise arrangements also fall into this category – the core content remains the same, but the local institution adapts the material (by translation, by including local case study material, or by customising the length or degree of difficulty of the material). The resulting course is often of very high quality, containing the best of both worlds – an international perspective with a grounding in local or national concerns. The UKOU has large programmes in Eastern Europe, Singapore and Hong Kong which demonstrate this quality of globalisation (Tait, 1996).

Finally, there are a range of collaboratively developed courses across all areas of the curriculum which encompass the perspectives of different cultures and approaches to the discipline. Gayol describes the activities of NADERN, the North American Distance Education and Research Network (Gayol, 1996), and the 'What is Europe' course authored by several European institutions is another example.

On most of these programmes the student body remains national, and therefore does not benefit from interaction with students or teachers from a mix of countries.

Global support structures

Very few universities have developed truly global support structures; the training programmes within globalised industries are probably closer to realising this aspect of global education. Whilst the Internet (in the form of electronic mail) provides a relatively trouble-free mechanism for administration, sending in assignments and receiving one-to-one tutoring, none of these features scale up to handling large numbers of students. Indeed, what we find most commonly, is that any course or programme operating globally, is only doing so with very small numbers of students (typically under 100, and usually closer to twenty). Frequently the course is administered and tutored by the course author – what can be categorised as a one-man band!

In many respects, the technology is not yet in place worldwide to manage large-scale global teaching. The aspects of support required in global courses include:

*   a system for many-to-many communication, such that students can interact not only with the tutor, but also with other students, and is accessible at reasonable speeds and reasonable cost on a global level;
*   a system for handling the electronic submission of assignments, both for the purposes of annotating, commenting and marking by the tutor, and for recording, monitoring and storing by the accrediting institution;
*   a system for marketing courses and programmes, handling registrations, fees and queries from around the world, preferably electronically.

Examples of these systems operating more or less successfully do exist, but certainly not on any large scale. Monash University has a system for managing the electronic submission of assignments (Mason, 1995); a number of universities use various computer conferencing systems on an international level for many-to-many communication (Harasim *et al.*, 1995) and a combination of Web pages, Web forms and email allow many online courses to be advertised electronically and for prospective students to register and obtain further information (Corrigan, 1996).

Scale of operations

If global education activity is confined to single courses, or even to one programme in a large organisation, it is not going to attract much serious attention. However, as the case studies in the second section show, there are a few organisations already offering a fair range of courses to relatively large numbers of students located in quite a few countries of the world. It is probably this fact more than any other which explains the current level of interest in global education. Many who have not entered the market are worried about the competition from these 'education invaders'; others view it as an opportunity and the opening of a whole new market.

While the number of truly global educational institutions is quite small, there are many global activities and events taking place within the higher education and training sectors. These can be categorised as:

*   global research projects, in which participants communicate, exchange data, and draft joint reports and books electronically, using simple email, audiographics, videoconferencing and CUSeeMe on the Internet;
*   consortia development activities, in which prospective partners develop mutual understandings which are intended to lead to global educational partnerships, or, as with the Globewide Network Academy satellite video-conferences, which foster a climate for global educational activity;
*   conferences held electronically, using the Web, computer conferencing, listservs or videoconferencing, either as a substitute for any face-to-face

meeting or as a method of extending access to those unable to attend physically (two examples are Faculty Strategies for Engaging Online Learners, a Web-enabled conference at http://www.umuc.edu/ide/strategies/conf.htm/, and Anderson and Mason, 1993);

- global programmes in which the administrators and/or the tutors communicate electronically, but the students do not;
- global videoconferencing in the workplace for such activities as presentations to all employees, for product promotions, job interviewing, or international project work;
- professional listserv discussions exist on the Internet in almost every curriculum area, and participation, though dominated by Western English-speakers, is nevertheless increasingly global.

The point is that these activities promote understanding and acceptance of telecommunications media and develop relevant technical and social skills in handling global communications. These are necessary components for the growth of global courses.

Global institutions

What I have presented so far is a picture, not of a revolution in the higher education sector, but more of a sliding scale from 'traditional' distance education, to international distance education, to online courses, to virtual universities, and finally edging to globalisation. Most of the operations are piecemeal, consisting of a good deal of flag-waving from senior staff, or idealistic visions of new educational paradigms from educational technologists, or financial officers rubbing their hands in expectation, but at the end of the day, a very few academics and trainers actually delivering something that could be called global in parts.

What would a truly global institution be like? By the strictest definition, it would not be more identified with one country or even continent than another; it would have accreditation, quality standards and administrative functions applicable in every country, and all courses available in all languages. Clearly this is a farcical notion, and I do not propose to apply such an unrealistic definition of the word global. However, because there are so very many institutions venturing into international educational waters, I think it is useful and legitimate to retain the word global for those institutions which are farther away from shore, as it were. The five attributes I have already used to characterise global education, represent a significant advance on mere international activity, although I admit that, by analogy with the business sector, the words multinational or transnational might be more accurate.

I turn now to the question of who is leading the globalisation movement. One response can be given with certainty: it is not the established institutions! This is not surprising considering their investment in physical buildings, their academic traditions and their self-imposed guardianship of quality, standards and research. One then looks to the newer, less prestigious institutions as being more flexible, more in need of making their mark and more desperate to find sources of income. Certainly this sector has adopted computer technology more wholeheartedly and is experimenting more readily with various forms of distance education. However, it faces many internal barriers:

- lack of appropriate staff training in order to teach with new technologies;
- lack of an appropriate reward structure to attract staff to adopt new methods;
- lack of resource to fund the development of global courses.

In fact, many of the 'one-man band' global courses do come from institutions (usually teaching face-to-face) where one or two early adopters are enthusiastically going ahead with little institutional support and much hard work, simply because they are committed to the principles or enjoy the actual practice.

The distance teaching universities are obvious candidates for leading the field in the globalisation movement. While the UKOU is one of the most prominent, many distance teaching institutions whether dedicated or dual mode, have some partially global courses – franchising systems, arrangements with one or two other countries, or a few Web-based courses being piloted to test the global waters. Nevertheless, these institutions also have entrenched attitudes, bureaucratic procedures and general inertia to overcome before launching themselves as global institutions. Re-engineering an educational institution to teach in new ways, with new media, to new kinds of students, is not an overnight task.

If one institution finds it difficult to gather the necessary resources, train its staff and provide whole programmes rather than odd courses, what about consortia? In fact, many of these exist both nationally and transnationally to share delivery technologies, course development, accreditation mechanisms, marketing and registration procedures and programme planning. Some of these are well-known, such as the National Technological University; many others are still in the early stages of consolidation and have not established a reputation. Without a doubt, consortia of all kinds will become the norm in the long term development and large scale build-up of global education. The complexities of teaching, administering, supporting and developing global programmes make this an obvious solution for the university sector to adopt in responding to the pressures for globalised education.

Another, slightly different, solution has appeared very recently, arising from the university sector but based on the new cyber-speak. These are the virtual universities, designed for a global platform and operating purely electronically. Some are idealistic and visionary in aim, such as the Globewide Network Academy (http://uu-gna.mit.edu:8001/uu-gna/index.html), although this originated in 1994, Spectrum Virtual University (http://www.vu.org) and Virtual Online University (http://www.athena.edu); others are avowedly 'for profit' such as Phoenix University (http://www.uophx.edu) and IMLearn (http://www.imlearn.com). The scale of these operations is variable: many of them on investigation prove to be working from one office; others have significant numbers (e.g. 2,000 registered for online courses at Phoenix University), although very few students will be non-nationals. On the whole, these are not universities in the commonly accepted sense of the term: they borrow academics from other institutions rather than fund their own established full-time faculty; they do not cover a full range of discipline areas; they do not fund research programmes and they do not support what is usually called an academic environment. Nevertheless, they provide courses which people want; they are capitalising on the phenomenal growth of the Internet and are trail-blazing the global pathways for others.

There exists one final model which might be said to be leading the field: the new educational providers. This group consists of organisations whose primary business is not, or has not been, education. Often they have services or products which have now become central to the delivery of global education. The obvious examples are the telecommunications providers, whether satellites, cable, telephone or combinations. Other examples come from the computer and software industries. The advent of these new providers offering professional updating programmes, adult education courses, life-long learning opportunities and just-in-time training resources to what has always been the market monopolised by universities and continuing education units, has caused ripples of alarm in all but the most un-reconstructed universities (Mason, 1996b). The natural advantages which these new providers have over the established education sector are:

- in many cases they control the means of delivery;
- they do not carry the academic 'baggage' of established institutions and are free from their bureaucratic and entrenched attitudes to education;
- as 'green field' sites they can set up systems geared specifically to a global market, rather than having to adapt existing procedures;
- they hire content specialists from traditional universities, but do not suffer the expense of supporting a research programme from the teaching revenues.

These points raise many questions about quality, accreditation, and ultimately the notion of graduate-ness and the purpose of universities. They are not issues specific to global education, nor are they new problems to the education sector. Several examples include the following:

- The McGraw-Hill Companies using their global distribution system have entered the content-delivery market, thus representing a significant threat to the traditional education sector. Through the McGraw-Hill World University, courses are offered in professional updating at certificate and degree level (http://www.mcgraw-hill.com/).
- The Global Telecom Academy is a brokerage service of distance learning

courses to supply training online for staff of telecommunications compa-nies worldwide. It is based in Geneva, and has just begun to offer a number of Web-based train-the-trainer courses (http://www3.itu.ch/VTC/gtu_gtti.htm).

- Microsoft Online Institute (MOLI) is an online education programme which provides courses in Microsoft product training and certification (http: www.microsoft.com/).
- Motorola University, Schaumburg, Illinois is part of the growing trend for corporate universities to move to the Virtual Campus model, by making strategic alliances with universities and online providers. For example, using the engineering courses offered by the National Technological University (NTU), Motorola has over 300 engineers in North America and Asia following masters degree programmes. By acting as NTU's main customer in Asia, they made it possible for NTU to establish an Asian service, and now other global companies such as Hewlett-Packard have joined, making it possible to justify one full transponder devoted to delivering NTU programmes in Asia (http:/www.mot.com/).
- Jones Education Company is founded by Glenn Jones to extend equality of opportunity for higher education to those unable to attend on-campus classes (see Chapter 8).
- Global Learning, a new venture into the education and training market by Deutsche Telekom (http://www.globallearning.de).

Conclusions

In this first chapter I have considered the pulls and the pushes affecting current interest in global education. I have laid out a number of criteria which define the phenomenon I will discuss in more detail throughout the rest of the book.

Although I have tried to dispel the impression that global education is commonly available, I consider the practice to be sufficiently developed to warrant a full-scale study such as this. Furthermore, I think the signs are that it is poised to expand and hence is a phenomenon worth analysing in its early stages. As the authors of a recent Australian report on 'borderless education' put it:

> There is no shortage of scholarly, journalistic, governmental or institu-tion-specific material on the impact of communications and information technologies, media influence, the globalised economy, or the future of higher education. There is however, an acute shortage of disinterested, thorough and realistic analysis of the intersection of these areas.
>
> (Cunningham *et al.*, 1997)

2 Media for delivering global education

Technologies for teaching at a distance

That computer technologies change and evolve more quickly than books about them can be published is an obvious fact. But educational use of computer and telecommunications technologies, or at least widespread take-up by institutions, is much slower, so that it is possible to discuss current delivery technologies and speculate about trends with some degree of certainty about the direction, if not the details, of global education delivery media. As I mentioned in the previous chapter, it is distance education, as presently practised usually on a national scale, which is the forerunner and first pioneer of global education. It therefore makes sense to study the technologies in use today, in order to assess the benefits and limitations of various media for the global education of tomorrow.

There are three broad categories within which current technologies that support global education can be divided:

- text-based systems, including electronic mail, computer conferencing, real time chat systems, MUDS/MOOs, fax and many uses of the World Wide Web;
- audio-based systems such as audioconferencing and audiographics, and audio on the Web;
- video-based systems which as videoconferencing, one way and two way, video on the Internet with products like CUSeeMe, Web-casting and other visual media such as video clips on the Web.

The implication of this list is that text, audio and video are discrete media. While this is partially true today, the evolution of all these systems is towards integration – of real time and asynchronous access, of resource material and communication, of text and video, in short, of writing, speaking and seeing. A good example of this integration is the CD-ROM, which combines elements of text, audio and video and consequently has tremendous potential as a stimulating learning resource. However, on its own, it lacks the significant component of person-to-person interaction. Furthermore, CD-ROMs are difficult and costly to update, and problematic as a global distribution medium. Recent developments overcome these shortcomings by integrating the CD-ROM with the interactive and updating capabilities of telecommunications. For this reason, I am including multimedia CD-ROM within the purview of my fourth, the ultimate integrating medium and the rising star of global education delivery:

*   the World Wide Web, which integrates text, audio and video, both as pre-prepared clips and as live interactive systems, both real time and stored to be accessed later, and furthermore provides text-based interaction as well as access to educational resources of unprecedented magnitude.

I will discuss each of these media in turn, looking at the main educational advantages and disadvantages and considering their potential for global course delivery.

Text-based systems

Without a doubt the most commonly used technology for communicating with students at a distance is electronic mail and various forms of group communication. Text-based interaction, whether many-to-many in conferences, or one-to-one in electronic mail, is practised at most institutions of higher education, whether students are geographically remote, or actually on campus. In fact, with the change towards the new majority (students who are older, or have some kind of part-time employment, or have family commitments or other barriers to attending campus full-time), many face-to-face teaching institutions use text-based interaction as a means of communicating with students, thereby reducing their dependence on physical attendance on campus at specific times. I tend to use the term 'close-distance education' to describe this new phenomenon.

Some institutions use standard electronic mail systems (which include the facility for sending messages to a group) to communicate with students at a distance. Those accessing from abroad usually use the Internet; those living locally may use a modem over telephone lines. The primary use is for students to ask questions of the tutor, but an additional use is the electronic submission of assignments, as an attachment to a mail message. This is the simplest and most accessible of all the telecommunications technologies, with the possible exception of fax.

More commonly in distance education, a proprietary computer conferencing system is used. FirstClass is a very successful product amongst educators, and Lotus Notes is common particularly in Business Schools and in training organisations. Web bulletin boards are also becoming very popular and most of the proprietary systems have integrated with the Web, so that conferences can be accessed from a Web browser. Computer conferencing systems allow students on one course to share discussion areas, to have sub-conferences for small groups, and to have easy access to all the course messages throughout the length of the course. Computer conferencing systems are slightly more complex than email, and they may require the student to have client software. A faster modem may be necessary as well, or at least highly desirable. Generally, the more extensive the system and the more advanced the facilities it offers (e.g. frames on Web bulletin boards), the more powerful the client's machine needs to be.

MOOs have something of a cult status and seem unlikely now to be taken up widely by the education community. A MOO is a text-based, virtual reality development from MUDs, an acronym for Multi-User Dungeon, a class of programs for playing dungeons and dragons over a network. From these real time, text adventure games evolved the MOO, which stands for MUD, Object-Oriented. Unlike conventional chat rooms, MOOs allow the manipulation and interaction with cyber-objects as part of the communication with other people. When integrated into the learning experience, MOOs can be used to create an environment in which students interact more directly with the course ideas than they would in an unstructured discussion.

The fax is most often used in the global education context for sending and receiving students' assignments. For example, the UKOU provides a fax machine to those of its UK-based tutors who have students in continental Europe.

Text-based systems can be divided according to whether they are primarily synchronous or asynchronous in use. More accurately, while the technologies usually support both, in practice one or the other is the primary intended use, and this influences the design of the interaction features. Figure 2.1 shows a screen from the FirstClass conferencing system in which messages are listed as separate items and comments on messages are apparent from the subject descriptors. While FirstClass includes a real time chat facility and some educational uses are made of it, the most significant applications of the system are asynchronous. Figure 2.2 shows a screen from Lotus Notes, which shows discussion threads more visually. Both systems now offer a Web interface.

Most text-based communication systems are used primarily to support students (with the *contents* of the course delivered through some other medium); however, some educators run 'online courses' in which the primary content of the course is the discussions and activities taking place amongst the students. As this technology has been in use on a relatively large scale for nearly ten years, and as some of these uses have involved students in many different countries, it is the most obvious area to study in this examination of global education. I will use examples from online courses throughout the first section, and will present several computer conferencing case studies in the second section.

One of the major advantages of text-based media is that they facilitate interaction for those using their second language. Most people are better able to write in another language than to speak. Furthermore, asynchronous systems allow time for reading messages slowly and composing a response

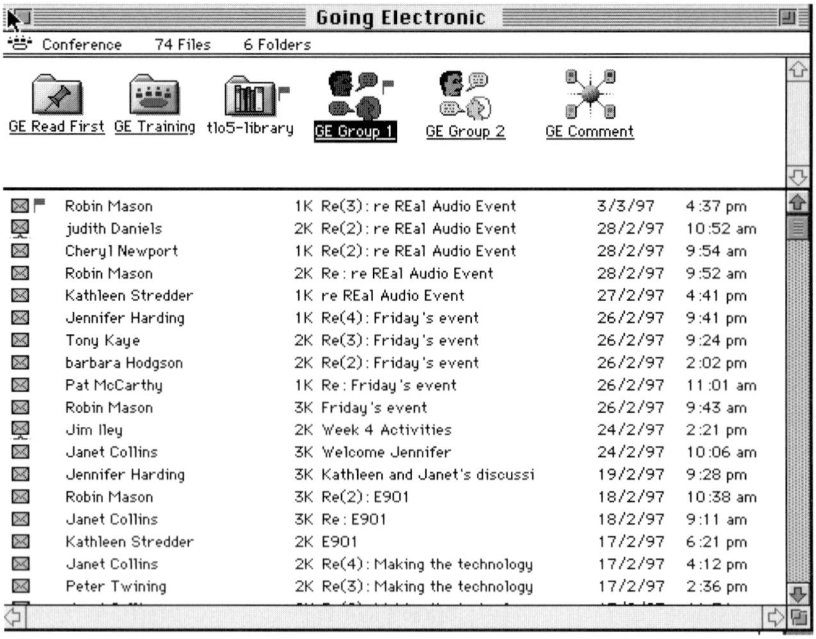

Figure 2.1 Screen shot of FirstClass

with the aid of a dictionary. Not surprisingly, there are a range of very successful asynchronous text-based programmes at an international level for second language teaching (http://128.172.170.24/gj/201/201.html). Usually they provide natural language practice with mother-tongue speakers, which is much more engaging and profitable educationally than artificial classroom practice.

Another primary advantage of any text-based system for global education is that many people worldwide can access them using a personal computer and telephone line from their home. In fact, although there are a few uses of real time chat or even computer conferencing in which students go to a study centre, campus computer room or training centre, most uses of these systems are asynchronous and from the student's own machine (whether at home or in the workplace).

My third advantage of text-based systems is rather more contentious. Much has been made of the equalising effects of textual communication – the concentration on what is said rather than who says it. While it remains the case that the disabled and the disadvantaged can participate without the usual judgmental reactions, text-based systems do not remove bias and 'advantage' – they merely shift it around a bit. Clearly those who have regular access (for example, from both work and home) or have no concern about the cost of access, are advantaged in terms of being able to participate in discussions more easily than those who have restricted access and cost considerations. Furthermore, those who have good writing skills tend to dominate by the very

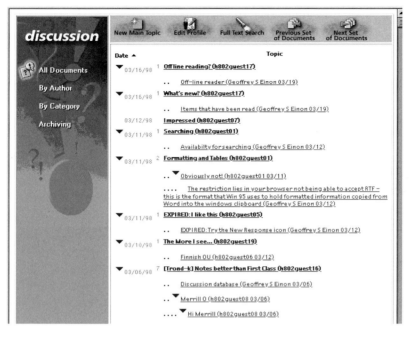

Figure 2.2 Screen shot of Lotus Notes

quality of their messages, in that less literate participants defer to them or simply are deterred from putting in messages themselves. Finally, the openness of these systems to anyone, any time, to make their opinion known, to respond to other viewpoints and to engage in dialogue, is true in theory, but in reality messages not following the main thrust of the discussion (i.e. keeping up with the on-going conversation) tend to be ignored. Abuses of the openness of the system, such as flaming (a jargon term to describe the all-too-common phenomenon of sudden heated confrontations between online participants often over misunderstandings due to textual communication), sexual harassment (also a common occurrence in online systems), and unsociable behaviour generally, have driven participants away and somewhat damaged both the image and the value of text-based communication (although this is much less prevalent in educational than social uses). So what was originally hailed as a new democratising medium, inherently more open than other modes of communication, has been shown in practice over time to be as flawed as the human beings who use it. Nevertheless, for some groups of people, text-based interaction allows access to education in a form ideally suited to their situation.

Audio systems

Straight audioconferencing using ordinary telephone lines is a 'low-tech' solution to supporting students in the developed world, due to the near ubiquity of the telephone in these countries. Many print-based distance education programmes use audioconferencing to help motivate students, and it has also been used for small group collaborative work at postgraduate level (Burge and Roberts, 1993). Nevertheless, there are few uses of this technology in group discussion mode (as opposed to simple student to tutor phone calls) in international programmes of distance education. Audioconferences are difficult to manage with more than half a dozen sites, although it is possible to increase the number of participants by having groups of students at each site.

An extension of pure voice interaction is audiographics: voice plus a shared screen for drawing or sharing pre-prepared graphics. Whilst this technology has had more extensive use in distance education, and examples of it being used between two sites in different countries do exist, I know of only one international, multi-site use in an educational application (Mason, 1994b). As with audioconferencing, audiographics use with more than two sites requires an audio bridge to connect all the lines together. There is no technical barrier to doing this internationally; cost is the primary deterrent. The term, 'audiographics', will probably die out completely as shared screen and multi-way audio are now possible on the Web.

Audio on the Web is a developing technology which many institutions are beginning to take seriously as an educational tool, especially when combined with various forms of real time, text-based interaction. RealAudio, for example, is a product which allows real time lectures on a global scale (http://www.realaudio.com/). Many distance education systems have involved sending audio cassettes out to students through the post. With audio on the Internet products like RealAudio, it is possible for large numbers of students around the world to access these 'broadcasts' in both real and delayed time.

Figure 2.3 is a screen from the UKOU's use of RealAudio to deliver a global lecture and discussion session with a series of experts. The interface which has been developed on the Web to support the events, is called the KMi Stadium, and provides facilities for slides associated with the lecture. Plans are in hand to develop a range of other tools to provide a greater sense of a global audience: indications of how many concurrent participants there are, buttons to show agreement or disagreement with the lecturers' ideas, etc.

> KMi Stadium is an experiment in very large scale telepresence. We are enhancing existing media and developing new media intended to give participants a sense of 'being there' at events of all kinds, including master classes, performances, tutorials, conferences, workshops, ceremonies, parties, jam sessions, recitals, industrial training sessions, university lectures, training on demand, town hall meetings, debates, and so on. For us, 'being there' is not primarily about Virtual Reality *per se*, although VR can certainly help. Rather, it is a question of capturing the right participative aspects of audience presence (such as applauding, laughing, shouting, asking questions, whispering to neighbours) and harnessing

those aspects to convey as much of the mood of an event as possible. We are interested in telepresence at both live events and on-demand replays, because we believe that both types of event are enhanced by a sense of the presence of others.

(Eisenstadt, http://kmi.open.ac.uk/stadium/)

Before leaving audio systems, it is worth highlighting another up-and-coming technology: voicemail. Currently this technology is being used by both distance teaching and campus-based institutions for mini-lectures, timely comments from the lecturer and for various types of assignments requiring a student response. I know of no international uses of voicemail systems, probably because of technical variations in national phone networks, but it is another 'low-tech' solution to adding interactivity and telepresence to the learning environment.

Video systems

Some educators feel that videoconferencing is not necessary in supporting students at a distance, and that audio, especially audiographics, works better because it concentrates attention on content rather than distracting the

Figure 2.3 KMi Stadium

Source: KMi Stadium and the developments from it, such as Pub Quiz, are the work of the following Open University staff: Peter Scott, Tony Seminara, Mike Wright, Mike Lewis, Andy Rix and Marc Eisenstadt.

learners' attention with the visual image of the speaker. For them, the significantly higher cost of providing video is not justified by the educational benefits. Others feel that we live in a visual age in which it makes no sense to restrict the learner to audio exchange. Video, when well used, contributes to the motivation of the student, makes the learning environment more social, and facilitates the delivery of exceptional learning materials in almost every area of the curriculum (see Mason, 1994a).

One-way video (with two-way audio) systems have widespread application in North American distance education and training in national and international companies. Many of these systems use satellite delivery to extend coverage. The educational paradigm of most programmes is the lecture at a distance, with students watching either from smaller colleges, in the workplace, or (most commonly) later on recorded video at home. A very great deal of distance training is carried out by videoconferencing, some of it internationally, using ISDN.

ISDN, which stands for Integrated Services Digital Network, is a set of international switching standards to which worldwide telecommunications providers are recommended to adhere. However, to date there is no universal agreement regarding the standards. As an integrated digital network, it can be used for more than one service, and in most educational contexts, this involves telephony (voice) and data (graphics or moving image).

Two-way videoconferencing over ISDN is beginning to take over from the one-way systems, and a number of multi-site applications are in use, for example, in Australia (Latchem *et al.*, 1994). Global interoperability of ISDN systems is still problematic due to the lack of agreement about standards, but international point-to-point and even multi-point videoconferences do take place daily in the workplace and are relatively frequent occurrences amongst educational institutions, although usually not directly for teaching. As with international audioconferencing, the barriers to extensive use are primarily financial, not technological.

Various forms of staff training are a particularly appropriate application of videoconferencing. For example, when an international company launches a new product, it faces the task of informing very quickly a wide range of staff, from sales personnel to technicians. Mercedes-Benz uses Deutsche Telekom's satellite-supported business TV service in conjunction with ISDN back channel technology. The programmes are broadcast to all Mercedes branch offices (by the end of 1997 this included thirteen European countries). The picture and sound from the studio are broadcast via satellite to each branch office with a dish, and each office is also connected back to the studio via an ISDN network.

The director sits at the 'master switchboard' in the studio and receives a signal every time a question comes in from a branch office. An ISDN connection is then set up between the studio and the person asking the question. This connection is simultaneously broadcast to the other branch offices so that everyone watching can follow the trainee's conversation with the instructor. The ISDN connection is cleared as soon as the question has been answered. As a result, charges for ISDN usage time are incurred only as necessary. The 'switchboard' serves as a control station for the ISDN back channels.

(Deutsche Telekom, 1996)

Mercedes-Benz can provide service training to approximately twenty times as many of its employees in the same amount of time as in the past.

Figure 2.4 shows a videoconferencing system called Socrates, designed by PictureTel specifically for the education market (http://www.picturetel.com/). Socrates is an integrated presentation station with a touch sensitive screen which allows the lecturer to see on one window of the lectern exactly what is being shown to students locally and remotely, and on another window to preview the visual aids prepared for the lecture or to browse the remote sites.

Despite the popularity of such systems, there are many educational technologists who disparage their use. The following is a particularly incisive critique:

> The widely held view that face-to-face teaching is inherently superior to other forms of teaching has spawned a major industry worldwide. It is difficult to believe that videoconferencing would have become such a major influence, especially in North America, without the intellectual complacency associated with the tyranny of proximity. The investment in videoconferencing has been quite staggering despite the widely held view that the lecture is a process whereby the notes of the lecturer are transmitted to the notes of the student, without passing through the minds of either . . .

Figure 2.4 PictureTel

The apparently unwavering enthusiasm for the proliferation of video-conferencing systems for the purpose of enhancing teaching and learning represents 'the tyranny of futility'. If most lectures are relatively futile from a pedagogical perspective, why spend vast sums of money promoting expensive futile exercises? A reasonable explanation is related to the rate of change, or lack thereof, in the educational context – a phenomenon known as the 'tyranny of eternity'. Educational paradigms tend to change direction with much the same agility as an ocean-going oil tanker.

(Taylor and Swannell, 1997)

Bates also concludes that instructional TV, in which video is used to lecture, rather than to supplement, enhance and enliven course content delivered in another medium, is ultimately not cost-effective (Bates, 1995, p. 115).

Streaming video on the Internet, however, is a developing technology which may have more lasting potential, precisely because it is more closely tied to the model of personal computing, just-in-time learning and Web-based resources, than it is to the notion of teaching and learning through traditional lectures. While technically feasible today, video on the Web as a global learning tool is restricted by the bandwidth available internationally. In theory it allows the image to be downloaded by remote sites in real time. What is more realistic today is video clips integrated with text-based material, to illustrate and highlight, rather than to deliver large amounts of live lecturing.

The Web

There is little doubt that the Web is the most phenomenally successful educational tool to have appeared in a long time. It combines all the media described above: text, text-based interaction, audio and video as clips, and, with somewhat less robustness, multi-way interactive audio and video. Its application in global education is unquestioned. Although access to the Internet is hardly universal, and large segments of the global population are more remote from access to it (whether through cost, or through unavailability at any cost) than they are to print- and post-based systems of distance education, nevertheless, vast numbers of people worldwide do have access, many from their home, and this access is growing exponentially.

The Web is merely a collection of protocols and standards which define access to information on the Internet. The three defining characteristics of the Web are:

- the use of URLs (Universal Resource Locators) which provide the addressing system;
- the HTTP standard (Hypertext Transfer Protocol) by which the delivery of requested information is transacted;
- the development of HTML (Hypertext Markup Language) through which links between documents and parts of documents are made.

Fundamental to the nature of the Web is its client–server architecture, whereby the client (Web software residing on the user's machine) requests a particular document from a Web server (a program running on a computer whose purpose is to serve documents to other computers upon request). Having transmitted the documents, the server then terminates the connection. This procedure allows servers to handle many thousands of requests per day.

Exciting new Web developments which add features useful for students and functions appropriate for course delivery are announced regularly. Some examples include:

* functionalities for supporting animation effects, thus making documents more dynamic;
* facilities for handling forms, and input to forms which are useful for course registration, evaluation, and other kinds of questionnaires and tests (see Figure 2.5);
* support for presenting tables, footnotes and mathematical symbols;
* features to simplify page development and editing;
* improvements to the search facilities;
* greater functionality to the communication systems linked to Web pages.

I have referred to the possibilities of audio and video on the Internet. One

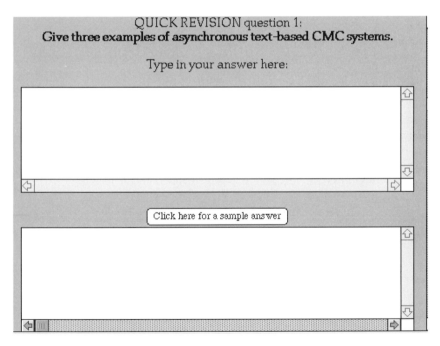

Figure 2.5 Forms on the Web

of the mechanisms for implementing this is through the programming language called Java and the HotJava browser:

> HotJava interprets embedded application <APP> tags by downloading and executing the specified program within the WWW environment. The specified program can be an interactive game, animation or sound files, or any other interactive program. Also, when a file or application requires particular viewers, such as for video, Java anticipates this and calls these viewers up automatically.
>
> (Collis, 1996, Interface 3)

Now that it is possible to download programs from the Web along with data, and to receive the appropriate software to handle the program automatically, the institution wanting to deliver course material can manage the maintenance and updating of any software required for the course. The student no longer needs to struggle with the installation of massive packages, and, furthermore, can use a relatively low cost machine – even a portable.

Synchronous versus asynchronous distance education

As is apparent in this description of different technologies for delivering education at a distance, some of the systems rely on real time interaction, while others can be accessed asynchronously. This difference has major implications for the design and delivery of distance education, as well as for the study requirements of the learner. There are advantages to both forms and, in the end, personal learning styles and the larger educational context determine what is most appropriate.

The following list details the major benefits of each mode in an educational context.

Asynchronous delivery

There are four crucial advantages to the asynchronous media and I have arranged them in descending order of significance:

- flexibility – access to the teaching material (e.g. on the Web, or computer conference discussions) can take place at any time (twenty-four hours a day, seven days a week) and from many locations (e.g. oil rigs);
- time to reflect – rather than having to react 'on one's feet', asynchronous systems allow the learner time to mull over ideas, check references, refer back to previous messages and take any amount of time to prepare a comment;
- situated learning – because the technology allows access from home and work, the learner can easily integrate the ideas being discussed on the course with the working environment, or access resources on the Internet as required on the job;

- cost-effective technology – text-based asynchronous systems require little bandwidth and low end computers to operate, thus access, particularly global access, is more equable.

Synchronous delivery

There are four equally compelling advantages to synchronous systems, although I am less confident of general agreement about the order:

- motivation – synchronous systems focus the energy of the group, providing motivation to distance learners to keep up with their peers and continue with their studies;
- telepresence – real time interaction with its opportunity to convey tone and nuance helps to develop group cohesion and the sense of being part of a learning community;
- good feedback – synchronous systems provide quick feedback on ideas and support consensus and decision making in group activities, both of which enliven distance education;
- pacing – synchronous events encourage students to keep up-to-date with the course and provide a discipline to learning which helps people to prioritise their studies.

Multi-synchronous course design

There are many technology-mediated distance teaching programmes which are entirely asynchronous (for example, those using print plus computer conferencing, or those using the Web for both course delivery and interaction), and others which are (almost) entirely synchronous (for example, those using videoconferencing for delivery and interaction). However, the trend is very much towards combining synchronous and asynchronous media in an attempt to capitalise on the evident benefits of both modes. The various permutations of media use and the amount of synchronous interaction included are almost as varied as the number of institutions providing distance education. Here are just a few examples:

- University of Twente, The Netherlands, an advanced level course about tele-learning developed and taught by Dr Betty Collis, consisting of face-to-face meetings plus extensive use of the Web. In 1996, the course had two students participating from outside The Netherlands, and all thirty-three students operating in their second or third language (http://www.to.utwente.nl/ism/online96/campus.htm);
- The Open University of Catalonia, Spain, currently offers courses to over 200 students in the Catalan region, beginning with programmes in business studies or educational psychology. Delivery mechanisms include print, multimedia CD-ROMs, videos and tapes; support media include electronic

mail and study meetings held twice a semester in resource centres linked up by fibre optic cable for videoconferencing (*Financial Times*, 3 October, 1995);

- Nova Southeastern, Florida, has an MS and EdD programme in instructional technology and distance education, using electronic mail and bulletin boards, and audioconferences and face-to-face 'summer institutes'. They claim to have graduates in fifty states of the USA and thirty-five foreign countries (http://alpha.acast.nova.edu/);

- George Washington University, Washington DC is a member of the JEC College Connection (see Chapter 8), which has a cable television network dedicated to distance education. The universities affiliated with JEC offer undergraduate and graduate courses in a range of subjects, using a range of synchronous and asynchronous media. Students outside the USA are sent video recordings (http://gwis.circ.gwu.edu/);

- The Fuqua School of Business, Duke University, North Carolina, offers a global executive MBA using multiple international programme sites for residential meetings, as well as email, bulletin boards and streaming audio on the Web. Desktop videoconferencing and CD-ROMs are also used occasionally (see Chapter 6);

- CALCampus, New York is an international online learning centre offering high school and vocational courses through the Internet. Two formats are provided: directed independent study (using text-based material sent electronically or by post) and live format (using real time chat systems) (http: //www.calcampus.com);

- School of Industry and Technology, East Carolina University, has an MS degree in Industrial Technology using real time chat, email, listservs, the Web and CUSeeMe interactive video (http: //ecuvax.cis.ecu.edu);

- The Virtual College, New York University, offers a small number of courses using digital video and video for Notes software from Lotus, which can be viewed in real time or downloaded for local storage and viewing (Reinhardt, 1995);

- The Sloan School of Management, MIT, Massachusetts has combined satellite videoconferencing (to Singapore and China) and Web materials and email communication with MIT students and faculty (Feller, 1995);

- OnLine Education, University of Paisley, Scotland, supplies course materials both in hard copy and on a computer, which along with a modem and printer are delivered and set up in the student's home. Live events take place both face-to-face and by teleconference, and students (in Hong Kong) communicate with their local tutor and with students in Scotland by email (http://www.online.edu/online/online.htm);

- Birkbeck College, part of London University, offers a global Web-based course on the Principles of Protein Structures which includes the use of a MOO to provide real time interaction (http://www.cryst.bbk.ac.uk/PPS /index.html).

It would be difficult to overstate the importance of flexibility to most distance education students. The pressures of modern life are such that most people demand programmes which allow them to fit their studying in and around many other commitments. None the less, it is equally the case that most people find synchronous events very beneficial for their learning. Obviously synchronous events raise even more problems in global education than in asynchronous distance education, because of the vast differences in time zones worldwide. Even though global videoconferences are held with some participants accessing at 'unusual' times, other solutions involve something which might be called 'fast asynchronous'. For example, the University of Phoenix operates an online text-based interactive system which is tightly structured to provide daily flexibility but pacing and feedback similar to synchronous teaching:

> Each of your class meetings and the accompanying class discussions will be spread out over a full seven days, giving you the weekends to get much of your reading and papers completed. As discussions build throughout the week, it is important to visit your classroom at least five days out of every week, but at times you choose and that best suit your individual circumstances. Before each week of class begins, your instructor will typically submit a lecture and review the assignments for the upcoming week. Then, throughout the week, he or she will be involved in the class discussions – providing expertise, guidance, feedback and answers to questions.
>
> At the conclusion of each week, you will be asked to provide a summary of the concepts covered. Based upon your summary and contributions to the class discussions, your instructor will let you know how you are doing and respond to any issues or concerns you might have.
>
> (Corrigan, 1996, p. 328)

Another solution might be called 'pansynchronous' to describe global events such as the KMi Stadium lectures, which many will access synchronously, yet others can access individually, or form groups to participate in on-demand replays any time thereafter.

Merging synchronous and asynchronous learning

Much of the above discussion implies that learning itself happens synchronously or asynchronously. In fact, what we have been describing are tools, materials and events which aid the learning process. What is at issue is how to meet students' needs, both for considerable flexibility in when and from where they access course material, as well as for the galvanising power of real time events to keep them on track. The following scenario by Collis provides a vision of how technologies are converging to satisfy both these needs:

With convergent technologies, this means that the subscribers, through their respective learn stations, may be able to see and talk to each other in real time; to review a real-time discussion that occurred earlier and perhaps make a non-real time follow-up contribution; as well as to participate in familiar asynchronous computer conferencing discussions. And even the familiar asynchronous computer conference will benefit from the possibility of multiple representational forms through the learner station – the tele-learner may choose to send her contribution by text, by voice, or by video clip; any combination of forms can be stored as an incoming contribution to an asynchronous discussion, waiting to be read, heard, or watched when the other participants come to participate in the discussion.

(Collis, 1996, p. 548)

What is so remarkable about the Web, and undoubtedly accounting for its popularity with such a diversity of users, is its capacity to bring together a range of otherwise disparate technologies, opportunities for designing courses, and competing providers of resources for learning. Its versatility can be summed up in the notion that anyone can publish and broadcast on the Web and thus reach large numbers of intended and unintended receivers. Users can choose to access learning materials, to communicate with fellow learners or to prepare their own personal pages. It supports real time personal interaction with its high telepresence through visual and auditory connection, yet it also provides outstanding facilities for asynchronous resource sharing and communication.

Regardless of how technology evolves in the foreseeable future, the Web has definitely set the benchmark against which any new media for global education will be measured.

Global technologies here and now

If the Web is so powerful and so successful, and so appropriate for global education, why are other media still being used? I will outline a range of reasons which apply to current conditions:

Inertia

Many institutions have been using other media for a number of years, have naturally built up professional expertise amongst the teaching staff, have developed courses to work with those media, have invested in hardware and software and have attracted a market to fill those courses. These are persuasive reasons for remaining with the status quo, while the Web technologies begin to stabilise and the early adopters have begun to develop some indicators of best practice. These arguments apply particularly to the large numbers of organisations using videoconferencing.

Approach to teaching

Studies show that the approach to teaching of those currently offering online courses by computer conferencing is very much a student-centred one (Berge, 1997). The environment of online text-based interaction, especially in asynchronous mode, lends itself to a facilitative teaching role, rather than to a didactic or authoritarian model. Online courses usually centre around collaborative activities, simulations and problem-based learning. This paradigm of guided discovery learning is the most obvious direction for Web-based courses as well, because of the combination of interactive multimedia capability and the many-to-many communication facilities, most of which will be used in asynchronous mode for some time to come. Consequently, the earliest migration on to the Web will be from those currently running online courses via computer conferencing, and perhaps to a lesser extent via real time chat systems.

Most of the courses currently operating over videoconferencing systems are founded on an expository approach to teaching. One of the key advantages of this medium, particularly to large-scale adopters, is that it does not disturb the traditional model of lecturers on the face-to-face teaching campuses (Mason, 1994a). While the introduction of remote students at other sites does have some effect on the teaching strategy (the need to acknowledge the remote sites while lecturing, the extra work involved in preparing visual teaching materials) and requires administrative and technical support in managing students at other sites, on the whole the delivery and presentation of the course material need not alter. Translating a lecture-based course to the Web, even assuming that clips of lectures were included, would require a significant re-engineering of the course, from an essentially didactic model to a resource-based model. Although many lecturers will welcome the opportunity to make this transition from videoconferencing to the Web, some of those in areas of the curriculum which are based on the accumulation of factual information and understanding, will find their old approaches to teaching much more difficult to adapt.

Development costs

Apart altogether from entrenched approaches and valued expertise, there is the cost of developing Web-based courses. While it is common to hear academics talking glibly about putting their lecture course on the Web, and it is sadly all too common to find teaching materials designed for a different delivery medium 'dumped' on the Web, in fact it is generally accepted that good Web materials need to be tailor-made for the medium, and should exploit at least the graphical if not the audio and video capabilities of the medium. Course content needs to be re-thought for the hypertext structure, for the possibility of collaborative group work, and for the opportunity of interaction with the course materials. As with CD-ROM, this requires a team approach, because the skills demanded range from content expertise and distance learning educational technology, to graphical design and broadcast skills.

It will take time for sufficient resources to be accumulated to produce high quality programmes on the Web across a range of disciplines. Nevertheless, many of these are in progress, and new courses are being offered on the Web every day.

Administering global courses

Systems such as PerformTrac from Computer Knowledge International, have been developed to provide basic administrative functions for computer or telecommunications-based courses, particularly those in the training field using CBT (computer-based training). In addition to online registration, scheduling and testing, the system allows the institution to determine how many trainees are accessing the CBT courses, how much time each individual spends working through the material and whether they passed the test at the end.

The kind of tracking which is important for the teacher in higher education, is slightly different. Tutors using text-based interactive systems need to know how often their students are logging on, whether they are contributing regularly, and who has read particular messages. This information is useful both on a daily basis throughout the course, and at the end to assess the overall success of the course. If students are being marked on the quality of their contributions to discussions, it is important for the tutor to be able to call up all the inputs of an individual student. Most Web-based conferencing systems do not provide this kind of support; some proprietary systems do have at least some of these features. Email and listservs of course have none of these.

Multiple media

Much of the evidence collected for this study points to the fact that even the leaders in the field of global education are committed to variation in their use of media. Institutions are wary of 'locking in' to one technology, and the best educators know that variety is a powerful teaching tool. Even though the Web does provide significant variety in teaching modes, there is still much to be gained from the use of print, satellite, cable, video and audio cassettes, depending on context, costs, access and flexibility.

Conclusions

I have provided an overview of the delivery media currently in use on distance education courses, dividing them into four categories according to whether they are based on text, audio or video. I have described the ways in which the Web integrates all three, so acting as the fourth category.

There is no perfect medium, however, and I have tried to highlight the primary advantages and disadvantages of these systems, based on the often conflicting needs of learners.

While it is still appropriate to talk about synchronous and asynchronous systems, this difference is falling away, as new developments aim to integrate the best of both worlds. The Web is the main technology to which all the others are converging, and its success derives from the fact that it can be 'all things to all people'. Except of course, if you do not have access or are never likely to be able to afford it! There will continue to be a place for 'lower-tech' systems such as computer conferencing and electronic mail, for audio and video cassettes, and the length of this period depends on how the Internet continues to be funded in the future. Equally, there will continue to be a place for distance taught courses, operating globally, but not using any form of computer or telecommunications technology. All of these technologies, even those which use unsophisticated computers or low bandwidth, are less flexible, more costly and more complicated than the technology of the book and 'snail mail'.

I have provided a range of examples of how various institutions are currently offering courses with several media to span the synchronous/asynchronous divide. Some of these applications are already operating with many of the components of a global system in place.

3 Pedagogy and global education

Introduction

In what ways does the growth of global education impinge on the traditional content and methods of teaching and assessment in higher education and training? Is the quality of global courses to be assessed any differently from national or campus-based courses? Do the cultural sensitivities and considerations of global teaching affect the curriculum? And if not, should they? Finally, what impact does the presentation of course material in the hypertext format of the Web, used extensively in global courses, have on traditional teaching and learning processes? These questions involving the content, curriculum, assessment and the methods of delivery are the subject of this chapter. As with other issues discussed in the book, they are not the exclusive concerns of global educators. They are part of a much wider debate about the future of higher education and changes in social attitudes; nevertheless, the assessment of global education practice cannot ignore these issues and indeed contributes to the debate.

Establishing quality in a new domain

When the UKOU was first established in 1969, there was considerable scepticism about the quality of the learning experience distance education could offer its students and consequently of the degree it would produce. Many critics said that the quality of a full-time, face-to-face taught degree was inevitably superior. Correspondence tuition, the only forerunner of the OU, had a poor track record. The OU, therefore, adopted quality measures as one of its highest priorities: considerable resource was devoted to the development of high quality instructional materials; teams of academics, producers, editors and educational technologists worked on the design, developmental testing and revision of the materials; external assessors from traditional universities were appointed to ensure that academic standards were consistent with the rest of the sector. The model was one of co-operative working with mutual assurance of quality and standards. Twenty-five years on, this approach has gone a very long way towards the establishment of 'supported open learning' as an accepted learning experience comparable to that of campus-based courses. Global education, I suggest, stands at the same threshold as the OU did at its outset: it has many doubters who condemn the very concept; it suffers from the activities of a few unscrupulous operators, and it has a huge task to establish quality practices and benchmarks. Furthermore, just as the UKOU was conceived in response to the emerging social and educational needs of the time, so global education is now evolving in response to a different set of social and educational needs.

Will the same approach to the establishment of quality standards also work for global education? Essentially this approach could be characterised as the wholesale adoption and adaptation of the standards of the traditional sector. One of the problems with this approach in the current climate is that the curriculum of the traditional sector, and hence the standards of best practice applied to it, are being questioned – not so much from within, as from without – by governments, employers and students-as-consumers seeking education and training as a passport to a job. Before addressing this issue of the changing demands and criteria for judging quality, I review briefly the arguments surrounding the quality debate in higher education.

The subject of quality assurance in education is a multi-faceted area, with a long history and many methods of measurement which have come and gone as pedagogical theories have cycled around from teacher-led to student-led approaches. Traditional measures of quality have centred around indicators such as exam results, numbers of class hours and even quantity of books in the library and number of students who are failed in the final exams! More recently, these measures have given way to quality processes such as contact opportunities between students and faculty, use of active learning techniques, feedback options, and level of services and resources to support learners. Even the definition of quality has been subject to re-interpretation, as absolute standards have been discarded for relative, context-based approaches:

> Quality in education is socially constructed and reflects the constructions of different periods and places . . . the attributes constituting quality can refer to intrinsic criteria (learning or performance as an end in itself) or extrinsic criteria, that is, goals or objectives external to the educational process.
>
> (Robinson, 1992, p. 12)

No issue so exemplifies the relative nature of educational standards as the subject of access. Where once the quality of an educational programme was defined by the numbers of students it turned away, in today's life-long learning climate, equality of access and extension of access to the traditionally disen-franchised are much more highly regarded attributes than exclusivity. Ehrmann makes a link between quality and accessibility:

> Project-based learning is of particular importance because it can engage

learners, and foster excellence among students who may not have done well in classes that relied chiefly on lectures and reading. Time-delayed exchange by electronic mail and computer conferencing also is of special importance for enhancing access, since many types of students seem to participate more fully in this medium than they are able to do in traditional face-to-face settings.

(Ehrmann, 1994)

The role of technology in the enhancement both of access and of quality is a significant element in the rise of global education. Yet the application of standards and performance indicators across national boundaries is even more problematic with global access. If we agree that standards are not objective, but relative to the context, to the needs of students and to their educational approach to learning, then this relative context must emerge out of particularly disparate elements with a global student body:

We can assure the students of the quality of our courses only if we listen to what they themselves need, be aware of where they are coming from culturally, respect the values, skills and life experiences that they own, and work towards solutions which, at the same time, don't compromise the educational and intellectual integrity of the unit of study we offer.

(Allen, 1993, p. 21)

The cultural and intellectual homogeneity of the majority of students on campus-based courses when exclusivity was the norm, has largely disappeared due to a range of social, economic and educational factors, but on global courses it has been replaced by diversity on almost every dimension. Sensitivity to individual learners, to their cultural-political context and fitting the course to this context – these are the new hallmarks of quality provision in multicultural education (Granger and Gulliver, 1996).

Changing demands on higher education and training

Most reports and inquiries into the future requirements of post-secondary, life-long learning predict a different set of demands from those operating even ten years ago. Future scenarios range from the sober to the radical; here are two examples:

[Students] will look for flexible, modular programmes of study with multiple entry and exit points that offer opportunities for credit accumulation and transfer and that recognise their prior learning and proven ability. They will place equal emphasis on personal enrichment and professional development; degree and short course opportunities are likely to be equally valued; demand for postgraduate and professional development programmes will increase rapidly. There will, as a result, be a further blurring of the boundaries between full-time and part-time study, between vocational and non-vocational education and between institution, home and work-based study.

(Open University, 1996)

and:

The new technological environment opens access to study across sectoral, disciplinary and cultural boundaries, which will quickly erode traditional ideas of the *course* of study: selective access, sequenced and carefully integrated content, and level-based progress rules that are pre-determined by the institution. On the contrary, curricula will be increasingly disassembled, modularized and customized to suit a wide range of clients requiring flexible delivery. . . . What constitutes a course will be increasingly negotiated between provider institutions, students and client groups.

(LeGrew, 1995)

Both of these suggest that choice, flexibility, and new skills will be fundamental to future provision. Others characterise the change required as a move away from content to process: ability to communicate, especially across cultures, ability to work in, form and lead teams, and particularly the ability to find, synthesise, and manipulate information. Many aspects of global education are wholly compatible with the direction of these changes:

- the cross cultural interaction fostered on telecommunications systems at the core of global programmes;
- collaborative work, small group interactions and joint assignments used on many global courses;
- the learning-how-to-learn skills which the Web fosters;
- the emphasis placed on communication between student and faculty, and amongst students in all online courses;
- the plethora of short courses, free courses and niche courses which are proliferating on the Internet.

In fact, it could be argued that global education is not just compatible with the direction of change, it is actively contributing to, if not leading the way. Given these aims of higher education and training, how should the assessment of learners be modified to reflect this change from content to process?

Assessment in the age of digital media

It is well known that few summative assessment systems attempt to assess the kind of non-cognitive, transformative learning goals suggested above. It is also well known that assessment arrangements define the curriculum in the eyes of the learner. Knight concludes therefore:

that the summative assessment arrangements say a great deal about the qualities of a programme. Grand aims without sophisticated assessment systems are virtually worthless. The assessment system is a powerful indicator of how seriously an institution takes its aims, showing whether the aims are an exercise in rhetoric or whether ambitious aims are taken seriously.

(Knight, 1996)

Another argument in discussions about assessment arises because of the greater ease with which students can plagiarise with digital media like the Web, online databases, word processing and CD-ROMs. The tutor cannot be expected to recognise unacknowledged material in students' assignments, when such vast sources are at their disposal. That this problem is continually debated underlines the fact that content-based methods of assessment are still being applied to conditions which demand a skills-based approach. This is undoubtedly because it is easier to design reliable assessment systems which test content rather than process. We have much less experience in assessing students' knowledge management abilities, the ways in which the course has transformed their thinking, and developed their skills in communicating and working with colleagues in the domain of the course content. Furthermore, such methods as do exist tend to be more time-consuming for tutors to mark (for example, successive, formative drafts of assignments) and are contingent upon a faculty dedicated to transformative rather than transmissive conceptions of learning.

Collaborative assignments

One way of tackling assessment in online courses has been project work, often including self-, peer- or co-assessment. The tutor workload is not significantly increased and, by including students in the process, assessment becomes part of the learning experience of the course – evaluating their own work and that of their peers, and commenting on the drafts of their fellows. In fact, collaborative projects and peer comments on formative assignments can become the central element of an online course with a student-centred approach to learning. A group of students on such a course in The Netherlands explain:

The students worked in small groups on an assignment to construct and redesign a chapter of a book, making use of the capabilities of the WWW. Not only the teacher could look into their work, but also their fellow students and everybody else who was interested. And the fellow students had to reflect upon each others' work, with the class as a whole dealing with design decisions. . . . Reflective learning was also an important aspect of the course. After every face-to-face session an assignment had to be made and every student had to reflect upon other students' work.

We all got comments and new ideas from our fellow students as well as from the teacher.

(Bos *et al.*, 1996, p. 35)

They go on to point out two other advantages to technology-mediated assessment: that the resulting projects were publicly available on the Web, thereby increasing students' incentive to produce their best work; and that the archive of projects built up from successive presentations of the course represents a valuable resource from which subsequent generations of students can learn.

There is every possibility that assessment on global courses could cease to be the proxy measure of student learning which it is in much higher education, and lead the way in being an integral part of the learning process, linked with the collaborative team work, with the interactive commenting and discussion, and with the development of resource-based learning skills. For example, my own institution, the Institute of Educational Technology in the UK Open University, is using the following kind of assessment on some of their global online courses: the first assignment of the block is a normal essay-style question with traditional marking by the tutor. However, for the second assignment, students revise the essay taking into consideration the comments from the tutor and from other students. In addition, students must comment on at least two essays written by their peers. In this way, students are learning the skills of analysing, commenting and revising written material. They must also be sensitive to the cultural, linguistic and educational differences of their peers whom they will never meet face-to-face. This kind of assignment is particularly appropriate at graduate level, and on courses for distance educators, such as these are. Using text-based electronic communications as the backbone of the courses obviously facilitates the exercise.

Roxanne Hiltz describes another model:

> Assign students to identify key concepts or skills in each module of the course, make up a question suitable for an exam to test mastery of this material, and answer each other's questions. Exams then actually include selections from the student-generated questions. Students are thus made partners in deciding what it is that is important to know related to course topics, and summarizing this key knowledge.
>
> (Hiltz, 1997, p. 3)

Another way of using a computer conferencing system to change the nature of assessment is to set a question for small group discussion over a period of several weeks. Students submit a given number of their messages for marking, and the criteria include such elements as the extent to which they have commented on the ideas of other students, and the degree to which they have integrated concepts from the course material (see Mason, 1995 for further details).

With real time systems such as audiographics and videoconferencing, it is possible to ask students to make presentations as part of their assessment. This is common in face-to-face education and training, and its extension to distance education through telecommunications facilitates the development of presentation skills as well as information technology skills.

Web-based assessment

The Web is also the focus of development of yet another form of technology-based assessment: multiple choice exams using Web forms, computer-based tutorials in which the tutor can monitor the students' progress electronically, and simulations with modifiable parameters which bridge the divide between learning and examining. These uses of technology do not generally involve collaborative work, and in this sense are closer to traditional assessment strategies. However, they facilitate the assessment process at a distance, which is obviously advantageous on global courses.

The Web offers a number of possibilities for assignments which encourage students to find, manipulate and synthesise information. For example, questions can be set which require students to search external Web sites, incorporate references and assessments of the information in their answers.

Knowledge management

More controversial than either of the two approaches discussed so far, is the notion of re-formulating the assessment system in order to test learners' abilities to find and use information, rather than to memorise and reproduce it. While there has long been much lip-service paid to this concept, digital technology makes it far more possible, and much more necessary! For example, on one course I tutored, which was built around extensive group discussion through a computer conferencing system, a student submitted a final project consisting almost entirely of extracts from other students' and tutors' messages. The 'art' was in the selection and the construction of a framework around the extracts.

This concept, often referred to now as knowledge management, is most clearly applicable in those areas of the curriculum which require the learner to have a broad overview of a large amount of information, and on courses which take a resource-based learning approach. It is less obviously applicable on undergraduate courses in disciplines where understanding is built on preceding ideas and processes which must be mastered step by step.

Examinations for a multicultural student body

Expecting students to attend examination centres around the world to write the traditional 'unseen' three hour paper in their second language, is the 'horseless carriage' approach to global courses. Continuing this practice devised for a homogeneous, campus-based student body into a globally dispersed multi-lingual context is a misplaced view of quality assurance, in my view. We need to explore more appropriate formats perhaps along the lines of a 'seen' exam, where the questions, suitably devised to gauge understanding and learning skills, are made available electronically and answers are returned within a pre-set period, say, twenty-four hours or perhaps one week. Rather than guaranteeing the identity of the student through physical means, peda-gogical means could be used – such as expecting students to weave in to their answers parts of previous assignments, online interactions and tutor feed-back. In other words, we need to integrate assessment into the curriculum, not tack it on at the end of the course. These are not cheat-proof approaches, but neither are traditional means, and at least giving students more time to prepare answers is more equitable to a multi-lingual student body. As Thorpe points out:

> Assessment is integral to the learning process and also one of the prac-tices which can have the most far reaching unintended consequences. Tasks which are misconceived may undermine achievement of the explicit learning goals which are the objective of the whole activity.
>
> (Thorpe, 1996)

Cultural considerations in global pedagogy

Studies of the effects of Western curricula and pedagogies imported to indige-nous cultures often conclude that, though there are educational benefits, this kind of post-colonial invasion undermines national initiatives which might be better suited to local needs, and leads to a continuing cycle of dependency on developed nations (Evans, 1995). Many non-technology driven examples of educational exporting from the developed to the developing world have taken place at all levels and across all types of curricula. The early history of this kind of globalisation has not been very positive. However, the kind of global educa-tion which is the subject of this study is not so much an exporting as a re-engineering of the educational paradigm to include people from many coun-tries, studying materials designed for a multicultural audience, using technologies which facilitate cross-cultural communication. Nevertheless, it is clearly the case that the leaders in the field of global education are predomi-nantly Western, the language in use predominantly English, and the pedagogical and cultural approach predominantly that of developed countries.

> Although there is a case for arguing . . . that there is a considerable diver-sity and diversification concomitant with globalisation, there is little likelihood of a myriad of small, local, traditional cultures being nurtured within globalisation.
>
> (Evans, 1995)

How can the new global education avoid the cultural mistakes of the old? One view is that the technology of the Internet and the Web is already breaking down traditional hierarchies and establishing a new kind of democracy about what constitutes knowledge. The traditional guardians of knowledge, the universities, are having to compete with other educational providers; anyone can 'publish' on the Web with apparently equal standing to the traditional publishers of academic knowledge. One effect of this democratisation is that Americans are becoming more attuned to the customs and cultural understandings of other countries at the same time as other countries are becoming more Americanised. This homogeneity makes the climate for designing global courses more favourable, although Spender calls this the academic equivalent of CNN (Spender, 1995, p. 140): learning by superficial sound bite, by global tokenism, by elevating cultural political correctness until it is nothing but an empty shell.

Another view is that globalisation is a phenomenon which is not going away, so its educational form should respect indigenous cultures and promote cultural diversity through dialogue and active learning opportunities. Homogeneity of the educational experience should be resisted along with the blurring of education and entertainment, and the commodification of instructional industrialism (Evans, 1995). The telecommunication technologies can be used to promote democracy, cultural plurality and small scale operations, just as they can support the forces of infotainment, domination and encroaching monoculturalism. Many critics claim that technologies in themselves are neutral; it is the people setting up the context in which they are used who determine whether globalisation brings benefits or dangers.

It is also a fact that there is great demand in developing countries for Western degrees and certification. Such people whom I have questioned feel that it is 'reverse colonialism' for Westerners to take the stance that 'we feel it is bad for you to want our degrees, so we will try to prevent them being available. Then you will be encouraged to develop your own, more appropriate systems'. With such attitudes, the West perpetuates its role of knowing what is best for others. The logical conclusion of this position is that organisations should enter the global education arena, as long as they do it with sensitivity to cultural differences, with attention to maintaining the quality of the educational experience, and with care for the learning opportunities which new technologies offer.

What do these pious aims mean in practice? How does one handle written work from foreign students which meets the content criteria but is really poor linguistically? This kind of problem is not restricted to global forms of education, but it is certainly easier to manage sensitively in a face-to-face context, especially if language support classes are available. At a distance, when communicating through text only, some practitioners have suggested that the student find a mother tongue speaker locally to read through assignments and advise on corrections. Similarly, is it possible to write course material which will not be misunderstood in any of a wide variety of cultures, yet still retains vibrancy, interest and relevance to an equally varied readership? In practice, most of the course developers I have questioned about this admit that while they make every effort to avoid jargon, obvious cultural and religious references, and case study material from one country only, they are essentially offering a degree/certificate/course from their perspective. It is not possible or meaningful to write culture-free material.

The UKOU Business School ran an internal staff development conference in October 1997, in which they brought together their course team authors, administrators and tutors working in many countries of the world (e.g. Russia, Africa and the Middle East), to discuss the cultural issues arising from the global take-up of their business courses (see Chapter 10 for a more detailed case study). I suspect this was the first such gathering on this scale to address the problems of adapting UK-based material, systems and pedagogy to a vast range of other cultures. I will highlight a few key ideas from the conference.

Course materials

While examples of cross-cultural misunderstandings are legion in the education sector, I will give one simple example reported by one of the tutors:

> In one English language exam, the recorded cassette said, 'it was raining again . . . '. The question in the exam paper said, 'What was the weather like – Good or bad?'. Naturally, the Africans all answered 'good'!
>
> (Kingsley, 1997)

The policy of adapting materials for the local context by substituting case studies, examples and papers from the target country, is not unilaterally appropriate, as the Russian tutor pointed out:

> Students from 'empire' organisations sign on for our courses to learn about how things are in the West. They use our materials as a blueprint for the new life, not as a way to develop their own management capacities in their existing lives (for example, they do not want boring Russian case studies to replace the lively tales of Western life appearing in our materials).
>
> (Thorne, 1997)

Pedagogical orientation

If many cross-cultural misunderstandings are avoidable, cultural differences in orientations to learning are much more problematic. The UKOU works within a liberal tradition of discussion, questioning, constructivist approaches to learning. Despite concerted attempts by tutors to explain the rationale behind this orientation in many countries, it frequently clashed with deeply-held contrary views, experiences and understandings. One tutor from Eastern Europe pointed out:

In a system where promotion is still driven more by political influence than merit, individuals are instinctively cautious in expressing dissent or disagreement. Individuals who come to us want to understand how our successful Western market based system works so they too can have the material benefits it brings. They see little point in resisting the transfer of this information by arguing about it. They do not pay such large amounts of money for the course in order to have an argument or to dissent.

(Morris, 1997)

Another tutor described the prevailing view in many non-Western countries as:

Listen, not speak; receive, not give – the teacher imparts the knowledge and the students receive it. It is a reflective approach to learning rather than an active one. In addition, this tradition is an oral one – written texts are less 'honourable' or 'trustworthy'. Lack of knowledge, experience or status will mean that contributions from 'the floor' are not welcomed by either the teacher or other students – it is merely wasting time.

(Kingsley, 1997)

Assessment

One of the issues of assessing students in a multicultural environment which arose during the conference was that of different expectations regarding the range of marks (e.g. from A through to F). For some people only A and B were acceptable marks; C and D were regarded as failures. Within the OU culture, C and D are used for the middle, standard work, and A and B reserved for exceptional work.

Some cultures regard Westerners as obsessed with time, and this attitude clashed with the practice of strictly controlled, three-hour examinations. One tutor resorted to telling all of his students that the examination was one hour before the actual starting time, in order to have the majority available at the 'right' hour.

Many tutors called for exam questions to be known a week or so in advance, especially because of language problems. The tutor for the Czech and Slovak Republics said:

unseen case studies can cause considerable problems in terms of grammar and structure, appropriateness and use of 'Western' cultural norms, and time spent using dictionaries to 'unscramble' the story in relevant local context.

(Farmer, 1997)

These tales of woe might lead you to despair about the cultural problems inherent in global education. I put this question to the conference: given this litany of clashes, misunderstandings and deeply-rooted difference, how do our courses continue to succeed in attracting such large numbers in so many countries? The answers lie in the combination of a very strong motivation for learning (and for Western accreditation of that learning), of the UKOU's reputation and of the quality of tutors working 'in the field'. For all the problems iterated during the conference, there were also many references to the benefits experienced by students (e.g. 'I've never experienced anything so mind expanding in my life').

Finally, and perhaps most importantly, one conclusion upon which there was general agreement, was that these differences can all be experienced by educational providers without ever teaching outside their own country. Cultural diversity within countries is now so broad, and approaches to learning are so varied, that many problems of language, misunderstandings, and pedagogical orientation are experienced just as profoundly on courses offered nationally and even locally, as they are on the global scale on which the UKOU operates.

Hypertext and the learning environment

The third pedagogical issue associated with global learning relates to the impact of non-linearity at the heart of some of the global technologies.

Hypertext is defined as the representation of information non-sequentially, using a network of nodes and links. The learning environment of print has conditioned us over many generations to process information in linear, sequential and static forms. The kind of coherence we have come to rely on to make sense of the world is largely based on narrative:

> Narrative is not simply the landscape of literature. Although this is where we are consciously most accustomed to experiencing it, it informs the paradigm of all of Western thought. We understand the world by telling ourselves, and others, stories about it.
>
> (Gibson, 1996)

While many examples of non-linear narrative have been explored by writers, television and film producers, they rely, in some sense, on the tradition and expectation of linearity. Similarly, although readers of a book may jump around within the text, and TV viewers 'zap' from channel to channel, the underlying framework assumes the coherence of linear narrative.

The world of hypertext is very different, and in its current manifestation on the Web, much of what has been fundamental to teaching and learning processes is confounded. First of all, the author of Web material cannot rely on how the user will arrive at any particular page, and therefore whether certain pre-requisite material has been studied. Some users may investigate the site thoroughly, following all links and examining every page. But even then there is no guarantee that they will do so in a predictable order. While there are hierarchical and linear structures possible on the Web, the user is often bewildered as to the extent of the site, and whether more unread pages exist. The fact that any parts can be updated and revised continually, contributes to the ephemeral feeling about the information on the Web. The linking structure on which it is based, both within a site and externally to other sites, means that one can easily leave the original teaching material and join another site anywhere in the world without being aware of it – the only indication is the changing url at the top of the screen. Having left the original site, the user enters a world with virtually no gate-keepers, as almost anyone can publish on the Web and the quality of materials is completely unpredictable. 'One reason we have readily accepted the reliability of academic information has been the process of checking that it goes through before it is made public' (Spender, 1995, p. 121). The reliability of public information disappears in the egalitarian free-for-all of the Web.

What impact is this break-up of traditional linear narrative having on teaching and learning? Given that global education is heavily dependent on the Web, will this impact be felt most sharply by global educators and learners? Of course it is always easy to judge the new and unknown as inferior to the tried and trusted. Let me consider the early indications of what kind of learning the Web does value. The most obvious kind of understanding that hypertext promotes is connections among pieces of information. A good designer of Web course material anticipates what learners are thinking about when working through pages and provides connections which will extend their ideas. Second, the Web validates the notion of many paths to the same conclusion, or of many ways of experiencing the same idea.

> All learning styles are valued equally. While educators may want to hold tenaciously onto particular types of learning – those associated with printed text – the World Wide Web is going to be telling users that every way of experiencing and interacting with information is equally valid. . . . Those in traditional positions of authority will be required to relinquish some measure of control.
>
> (Gibson, 1996)

Gibson goes on to say that different paths through material will result in different conceptualisations, and some paths will be better than others, but the point is that it is the learner who will decide this, not the teacher. Third, the concept of coherence may evolve from single to multiple layers of experiencing text. Users will need to actively construct their own story by interacting with the materials. They will come to expect multiple voices, multi-dimensional ways of viewing the information; quality will be related to the richness of associations, connections and alternatives. Spender compares this kind of narrative to the oral tradition of story telling:

No story will be set, closed or an enduring reference point. There will be no unchanging wisdom to be transmitted. Rather, 'stories' will be fluid and changing, as they often were in oral culture. There will be multiple versions as users make their own marks and create new paths and options.

(Spender, 1995, p. 90)

In this new dispensation, the learning environment is a theatre where an active performance is always going on in which students and teachers are both actors and audience, collaboratively constructing the story of the discipline.

Conclusions

I have tried to illustrate a number of ways in which the content of global education courses will be different from the traditional paradigm and will require different measures of quality assurance. The technology of delivery is central to this difference, defining a new approach to teaching and learning centred around interaction, collaborative activities, and knowledge management. The systematic separation of knowing and testing will give way to processes associated with personal transformation, social construction of knowledge, and cross-cultural communication.

Yet the technology must not be the driving force in defining the shape of global education. What the technology can do is not what it has to do. By focusing on our pedagogical aims, we can keep technology a servant, not a master.

Many educators who want to capitalise on the real benefits of global education share a vision of using technology to become more attuned to cultural contexts, to listen and respond to individual differences, to provide multiple opportunities for interacting with information, and to develop a curriculum responsive to the needs of the twenty-first century. We should expect the content and pedagogy of global courses to be different.

4 Students and technology-mediated education

The promise of technology-mediated education

Because global education is in its infancy, there are very few evaluation studies of the effects of this kind of programme on students. However, research on the value of technology-mediated courses delivered to distance learners is well developed and it is possible to extrapolate from observations and recommendations in this body of literature some of the issues which apply to global distance learners.

The vision which technology-mediated distance learning has been said by so many to offer students around the world in the twenty-first century, is generally expressed as follows:

> The technology of the Internet/WWW, and especially online education, has the potential to transform how we work and learn. It can truly move us into the concept of lifelong learning, which prior to now, we've only understood peripherally. We still divide our work, learning, and living into distinct and separate categories that very rarely, if ever, cross over and inform the other. . . . People can work with information and, through dialogue and discussion with others around the globe, construct knowledge. The nature of knowledge and research will be redefined. Education and training can be more timely, more relevant, more here and now.
>
> (Dewar, 1996)

It consists of the following advantages:

- flexible in terms of time and location of access;
- self-directed in terms of choice of learning paths;
- interactive in relation to tutors and other students;
- relevant in terms of its integration with work and with individual learning goals.

In many Western countries, working adults and mid-career professionals have overtaken the traditional student population as the largest growing sector in tertiary education. A variety of distance education programmes have developed in response to the needs of this 'new majority'. Central to the provision is usually synchronous or asynchronous interaction with the tutor and other students. Collaborative activities, joint projects and small group discussions have also become staple elements in online courses. Furthermore, the Web has enabled many instructors to develop resource-based, self-directed course materials as part of a student-centred approach to teaching or as an attempt to appeal to adult learners.

In this chapter I will examine the extent to which this vision is a reality for students of current technology-mediated courses. I try to extract from a wide range of evaluation literature the elements of good practice which will apply to global courses delivered using the same technologies.

Student feedback

There can be little doubt that adult students are demanding flexibility in the provision of postgraduate and professional updating courses. Even undergraduate campus-based students – in the USA particularly – welcome programmes which allow them to access computer-based teaching materials in their own time. (This is due to the fact that many have part-time jobs to pay for their tuition, and to a growing disillusionment with large lectures in which virtually no interaction takes place.) Studies of interactive television courses show that many students record the lectures to watch in their own time, thereby sacrificing interactivity to gain flexibility (Mason, 1994a). Even Web-based materials, though flexible in terms of time of access, are not flexible enough in terms of study habits for some students: the need to fit studying in between the main demands of job and family mean that some students print out Web pages and even CD-ROM materials in order to read them on the journey to work or anywhere without access to a machine or network (Mason, 1996a).

But this over-riding demand for flexibility leads to one of the problems with technology-mediated courses: the need for high levels of motivation and time management skills for busy adults to keep up with the course. Without the demands of synchronous activity (having to attend a lecture), students often fall behind. High drop-out rates have always plagued 'traditional' paper-based correspondence education programmes. Technology-mediated distance courses have higher retention figures on the whole, but purely asynchronous, self-paced courses often suffer from a minority (about one third) of inactive students who rarely contribute messages to the online discussions or who do not keep up with Web-based exercises and tutorials (Goldberg, 1996).

Related to this inability many student have to pace their work, is the problem some have with taking responsibility for their own learning. Faced with a resource-based course in the form of readings, Web materials and a study guide, for example, some students will thrive on the opportunity to pick and choose, follow interesting leads, and concentrate on what is most relevant to their context. Other students will flounder, complaining that the instructions are not clear, and they don't know what they are supposed to be doing.

> Our experience with student use of **WWW** information is that students demonstrate a great range of enthusiasm and persistence in seeking materials, and the poorer students (those most in need of supplemental enrichment) are the least effective at ferreting out the necessary information.
>
> (Lin *et al.*, 1996, p. 174)

One of the benefits of Web-based courses is said to be the way in which the materials build up from one delivery of the course to the next, making a richer resource for students in subsequent years. Yet one instructor reports:

> While I had hoped that students would avail themselves of materials from the previous course, most (66 per cent) made no use of past materials. Of those that did, the primary use was to look at past student homework assignments for ideas.
>
> (Rebelsky, 1996, p. 279)

In short, there is a mismatch between the hype about resource-based learning and students' skills or interest in taking advantage of rich resources.

Courses in which asynchronous messaging plays a large part often leave a significant number of students overwhelmed by the amount of information and the mass of messages to read. A typical response by students who lack confidence in their ability to process and critically access information is the following: 'FirstClass offered somewhere to find information, but there were too many ideas and they may also be wrong' (Bennett, 1996).

Despite this litany of negative findings about students' abilities to cope with student-centred courses, it must be stressed that most evaluation studies consistently report that the majority of students are enthusiastic about technology-mediated courses. The following quotations from students (some adults, some traditional undergraduates) who have taken courses largely delivered electronically, are typical.

> The online education program gives me the flexibility to adjust my class schedule to better fit my work and home life. It also gives me the ability to focus my concentration on the areas of the material where I am having difficulty and reduce the time I invest in areas where I have a clear understanding of the information.
>
> (University Online, http://www.uol.com)

> The voicemail system really works. I talk to my professors and get to share ideas with the other students in the program. I feel part of the class although I'm not physically in the same room.
>
> (Student of Jones Educational Company)

You appreciate other people's viewpoints. It makes you think about different arguments and the issues that you've missed.

(Thorpe, 1996)

Furthermore, there is evidence from teachers of technology-mediated courses that the quality of the student learning can be superior to traditional methods of course delivery:

> I do think it is worth mentioning that this was, without a doubt, the best composition class I have ever taught, the student writing was the best I have ever incited, and the students themselves were extremely diligent, self-organizing, and enthusiastic about the class, often running class sessions on their own and often meeting after hours to do small group work.

(Unsworth, 1994)

A global student body

What lessons from the literature on student reaction to technology-mediated education can be extrapolated and applied to global education? It is well known that access to the Internet is currently, even in Western countries let alone others, highest amongst those already educationally advantaged. This same constituency will undoubtedly provide the first students to 'self select' for global courses in both developed and developing countries. It is easy to predict the likely profile of the global student body over the next few years:

- they will be highly motivated and relatively good at self-pacing;
- they will be in employment and perhaps looking to change careers;
- they will probably already have computer skills and will be curious about learning in a technology-mediated environment.

In short, the first global cohorts will be the most suitable types of learners for the demands which distance and technology place on students. The majority of global programmes will undoubtedly be postgraduate and professional updating courses, rather than undergraduate, at least initially. Furthermore, the areas of the curriculum most appropriate for a global content (where perspectives from a global student body, or material reflecting global considerations, is relevant), will be the first showcase successes.

Flexible access to the course materials will be fundamental as students will be located in different time zones around the world and in countries where the postal system is not reliable or appropriate. The primary delivery of the course will be asynchronous. Synchronous contact will take one of two forms: real time chat sessions (either text or audio), or occasional residential or videoconferencing sessions.

A programme which encourages students to integrate their work experience with the course will also be an important part of global courses. The materials will need to be adaptable to a wide range of contexts and this will frequently be catered for by providing learning resources and setting assignments which students can apply to their own situation. Given the even greater sense of isolation global students will feel, electronic interaction and support systems will be the key to establishing a vibrant learning environment.

Telecentres

The picture I have painted of the 'typical global student' is, of course, a very elitist one. While I think that this is where global education will be most successful initially, its future is surely much broader. If access to equipment is one of the current barriers, we can consider one of the current solutions at a national level – the telecentre concept. While these operate slightly differently in various countries, the basic model is similar to the Australian version described here:

> The Telecentres are small enterprises in rural communities in Western Australia that contain a range of information technology and telecommunication resources to provide members with increased education, training, business and employment opportunities. The Telecentres have emerged from a need to provide increased access to education in rural regions. They are owned and run by rural communities with small amounts of financial and administrative seeding support from a central government agency.
>
> (Oliver and Short, 1996)

McLoughlin (1994) reports that Australian users of telecentres are positive about the educational benefits, and courses delivered by interactive television (with two-way audio), audioconferencing and computer conferencing have all proved successful. Oliver and Short note another aspect of the success of the Australian examples:

> An interesting trend is the level of participation of rural women. Enrolment in vocational courses among rural students has traditionally been 80 per cent male and 20 per cent women. The membership and participation in Telecentres has shown a direct swap of these numbers. The Telecentres have proven to be extremely popular among the women in rural areas who make up 80 per cent of the enrolments.
>
> (*op. cit.*, p. 241)

Could the concept of a centre for shared resources be applied on a global scale? The beginnings of this possibility can be studied in Europe, where the concept has taken the form of Euro Study Centres, situated not in rural areas, but in large conurbations where students can access technology-mediated courses from any European distance education provider. The centres house various kinds of networked equipment for both synchronous events and asynchronous study and access, and a facilitator is available for basic local support.

Still in their early stages, these centres currently attract many expatriates who want to take courses offered by their mother country, delivered in their mother tongue. The greatest number of users are UK Open University students, because the UKOU is the most developed in its use of telecommunications technologies of any of the European distance teaching institutions. There is little activity so far which could be called truly trans-European.

So what we can conclude about students' reactions to technology-mediated global education is based on the needs of an elite group of early adopters and the successes which local initiatives have produced. However, if the initial enthusiasm of the few is to be turned into a self-sustaining market and a successful learning environment for the longer term, there are actions which tutors and course designers must take to overcome some of the worst problems technology-mediated courses have encountered in their non-global form.

Technology-mediated strategies for engaging students

Ehrmann (1991) sums up the issue of good practice in technology-mediated courses as one of increasing student engagement with the course. The single most reliable determinant of learning outcomes in college-level courses is the time and energy students put into their studies. How can teachers and course designers increase either the total amount of time or the effectiveness of the time students voluntarily spend studying? Evidence from practitioners who have been teaching online for some years, and from students who have taken online courses, suggests the following:

*   providing good structure to online courses;
*   training both students and staff in the use of the technologies;
*   varying the media which deliver the course content and support interaction;
*   developing approaches which cater to the individual needs of students.

I will discuss each of these suggestions in turn.

Structure

The novelty of text-based interaction, when it was first introduced in distance education (Mason and Kaye, 1989), was such that many practitioners fell into the trap of thinking that providing students with a user-friendly system and a lively tutor/moderator were the keys to successful, educational discussions. As experience with these systems in a very wide variety of educational contexts has accumulated, and as evaluation studies have reported findings from learners – particularly from those who are not overly enthusiastic about the medium – there is increasingly realisation that the online learning environment needs considerably more structure than the early proponents anticipated in order to produce optimum results for all students. The concept of 'lurking' is computer conferencing jargon for describing participants who, for a range of reasons, only read messages and rarely venture to become active by inputting their own messages. Klemm and Snell explain:

> As usually practised, learning [with computer conferencing systems] takes the form of 'discussions' among several or more participants. Commonly, many students 'lurk' in the background without making contributions. Our experience in teaching four college courses and monitoring three others in a computer conferencing environment convinces us that such discussions are not very rigorous and that the quality of instruction suffers unless the teacher takes special care to create a more challenging learning environment. We have learned that instruction can become much more effective if students are required to DO something instead of just talk about it and to work together as a team to produce academic deliverables.
>
> (Klemm and Snell, 1996)

One way of providing structure is collaborative tasks carried out in learning pairs or small groups. Students may be asked to prepare a joint statement about some issue, or a joint report about an article, or they may take different roles in a simulation or debate. These activities need time boundaries set by the tutor.

Another element in structuring online activities is careful separation of discussion areas. Students who are very short of time and therefore very focused in their study goals, need to be able to find the messages which pertain to their activities quickly. Important messages from the tutors must be easily identified from messages of a social or peripheral nature. There should be places for students who want to socialise; there should be opportunities for those who want to participate as fully as possible in 'enrichment' discussion, but equally there must be clear routes for those who only want the 'compressed version'. Forming students into small groups (and perhaps changing around the members over the duration of the course) is usually the solution to conferences with too many messages and complaints from students that they are overwhelmed with comments from the same clique of active participants.

Does this kind of teacher-directed structuring undercut the notion of student-centred learning and the development in learners of self-pacing and self-directed learning skills? Experienced online educators are aware of this contradiction and talk about finding a balance between, on the one hand, providing an efficient learning environment for busy students who are at one remove from the presence and motivating force of the teacher and other students, and on the other, acting as a facilitator for students to develop the course in their own directions. Finding this balance for any given context is one of the creative tensions which all good teachers thrive on – adjusting this balance for the online environment is part of the art of teaching online.

Tutors of an online course run by the Institute of Educational Technology at the UKOU have experimented with the structure/no structure diad in the following way: in one group the tutor allowed the students to divide up the tasks of a group exercise themselves; in another group, the tutor asked for volunteers for each of the roles; in the third, the tutor assigned each student to a particular task. Each group consisted of about eight to ten students. After trying this experiment over a number of course presentations, the three tutors have decided that 'more rather than less structure' works best, and they have settled on the volunteer method as providing the greatest task efficiency with the greatest scope for student initiative.

Training

It is obvious that training in the use of the particular technology, both for the students and for the tutor, is an essential element of technology-mediated courses.

> Research data indicates that student attitudes toward technology often evolve as student familiarity with the technology increases. Students new to a particular technology may initially exhibit some concern about the role of technology in the learning experience. If this occurs, these students typically demonstrate a reluctance to actively participate in the distance classroom. However, a series of studies has shown that familiarity with technology over time erodes anxious feelings.
>
> (Reid, 1996)

There is another element to training which some courses have begun to take seriously: training in the educational methodology of the course. For example, a course which is resource-based, might include exercises in how to scan and search for materials, how to cope with large amounts of information, and how to focus on critical themes in an article (see, for example, Macdonald and Mason, 1997). Courses which rely on collaborative work and group inter-action might help to develop these skills in students at the beginning, by using pairs with simple joint tasks and building up to larger groupings with more complex team projects.

As technology-mediated courses rely on skills of team work, resource-based learning, self-pacing and information handling, it is important for teachers to address the development of these skills in students, along with the actual content of the course. By assuming students already have these skills, or not realising their importance to the learning experience, teachers are creating more barriers to technology-mediated courses than are necessary.

Coherent programmes

It is unreasonable to expect that the kinds of fundamental changes in approaches to study and learning, which technology-mediated courses are instigating, will have measurable outcomes after one course. Students develop patterns of working with information and form attitudes to learning from various media over long periods. What is needed is a sustained programme over many courses, which offer a broad range of opportunities to develop new skills, change attitudes and adapt habits to the new demands. Compare the kind of processes a student must go through to excel in a lecture-based course with regular assessment exercises and a multiple choice exam, to the kind of processes the same student must go through to excel in a Web-based asynchronous course with team marked assignments, readings to be found on the Internet and a final grade based partially on contributions to online discussions and activities. Even if the content of these two courses is roughly the same, it is hard to imagine many students who could do equally well in both contexts, or who would want to switch from one kind to the other every few months.

In fact, many first-time global students face just such a shift in learning demands. They will probably have been conditioned by a teacher-centred educational system which offered little room for meaningful interaction with the tutor and probably no collaborative work with other students. Students from certain countries may have no experience of questioning the views of the teacher. Older students will probably have a broader perspective from their experience in employment, but becoming a 'student' again often makes perfectly confident, competent adults adopt the outlook and expectations they had whilst in the classroom. It is unfortunately all too common at the end of an online course to see comments from students such as, 'I was just starting to get the idea of this course and now it is finished'.

Although there are beginning to be whole programmes of study offered partially or fully by telecommunications technologies, the most innovative tend to be 'one-off' courses lasting one year at best. I know of no evaluation of students taking a full undergraduate degree by technology-mediated courses. Until global courses can reliably draw upon a pool of experienced self-directed learners, we must provide support and training in how to be a learner in the new environment.

Student guide

This chapter aims to look at the globalisation of education from the students' point of view. So far I have been considering a range of pedagogical issues which affect students of online courses. I want to turn now to more practical issues and conclude with a checklist of issues for the student thinking of enrolling in a technology-mediated distance course, to bear in mind when considering a particular course.

What does it feel like to be studying a course written for a different cultural audience with a different pedagogical orientation? Imagine registering for a course from an institution completely unfamiliar, for which there is no local, tacit understanding. The following list suggests the kind of critical information the global student needs in order to make an informed decision before registering.

- The aims and objectives of the course: before registering for a course, the student should be able to access a course outline which includes a list of aims and objectives, information about the length, level and assessment scheme, and ideally details about when the course was developed or updated. Lack of such information, or failure on the part of students to consider it carefully, leads to dissatisfaction and drop-out in any form of distance education. In a global environment, where there is no 'grapevine' of advice about courses, this information is even more critical.
- The delivery media of the course: students should be encouraged to consider how they will access the materials, when they will fit the studying into their daily routine, and whether they are willing to adjust their learning style to the demands of a particular course. This is the beginning of the training and support that students need for learning in a mediated environment.
- The institution offering the course: clear information must be provided about the credit rating of the course and whether it will be possible to transfer the credit to another institution. Arrangements about local support mechanisms for technical difficulties, counselling and interaction with the tutor and other students, are concerns students should investigate before enrolling.
- The cost of the course: finally, as one of the case studies shows, students should consider whether there are any hidden costs of the course over and above the stated fee, such as equipment, telephone charges, set books or extra readings, travel to resources or meetings.

Global education is in the 'cottage industry' phase of development. As numbers are still small, and the concept still novel, most institutions and global teachers are sensitive to the needs of each individual learner. This sensitivity may involve an awareness of cultural difference, but also of learning style, level of confidence with the technology, and engagement with the content of the course. As the numbers begin to increase, how will the extra demands of a global student body be met? Some large scale international programmes already exist, notably through the UKOU and through various corporate training schemes. The case study in Chapter 10 looks at this issue in detail. The advantage of a large scale provider is a certain reliability about the quality of the product and a greater chance of a whole programme of study being available, rather than a one-off course. Another growing phenomenon on the global horizon is brokered or collaborative schemes in which materials developed by one or several institutions are offered or tutored locally by another institution. Here the prospective student should be quite clear about the division of responsibilities amongst the various institutions for accrediting, updating, assessing and supporting the learner.

Conclusion

Students generally like technology-mediated courses. They value the opportunity to study without having to attend lectures at a set time and place. They usually find the support of other students invaluable in overcoming a sense of isolation and in providing a range of perspectives on the course issues. Some find resource-based learning methods a liberation from the limitations of teacher-directed approaches. On the other hand, other students require the structure and imposed pacing mechanisms of that approach in order to maintain engagement with the course.

A global student body will probably experience similar benefits and problems, as the first guinea pigs on global courses will be similar in profile to those currently taking technology-mediated courses. Mechanisms for improving these courses for students involve providing carefully crafted learning environments to meet the range of learning styles, training in the processes and skills of technology-mediated learning, and extended programmes in which students can adapt to the new demands and discover the real educational benefits of this form of learning.

5   Organising a global education programme

Re-engineering the organisation

It is fashionable to talk about re-engineering the traditional campus in order to respond to the changing demands of the Information Age.

> As we enter the 21st century, changes in populations as well as in technology will lead to changes in the nature and structure of higher education. Increasingly, student populations throughout the world are older, employed, and more widely dispersed. As a result, the needs of students have changed. No longer are they adolescents making the transition to adulthood, instead, they are adults who need practical skills that can be used in their work. Institutions of higher education must adapt in order to meet the needs of these students or be replaced by commercial interests that are willing to do so. Fortunately, new technologies allow for changing the way in which education is delivered so that it will meet the changing needs of students both domestically and internationally.
>
> (McIntosh and Oliveras, 1996, p. 1)

In this chapter I will describe the way in which some institutions are adapting to these changing demands and investigate the issues involved in making these changes. Many of the forward-looking institutions (both academic and commercial) are providing their courses on a global scale. The latter part of the chapter examines a number of structures for managing and supporting a global teaching programme.

Bacsich argues that the development of technology-based teaching and learning is a logical consequence of re-engineering the teaching process:

> and in that re-engineering it is more than likely that elements of outsourcing, delayering and the other normal consequences of re-engineering will take place. Thus I think that all universities will go along the virtual dimensions. Those interested in world-wide presence will go further along the dimensions.
>
> (Bacsich, 1997a, p. 7)

He further contends that cutting the cost of teaching should not be the driving factor in this process – merely a result. I would add to that a warning against allowing globalisation of one's teaching programme to drive the process of re-engineering one's organisation – although again it is a typical result of it. The necessity of re-thinking the whole system of higher education results from the fact that the function it was designed to fill has ceased to exist. The old function was to provide mastery of a body of knowledge and a complete preparation for a lifetime career. The new function for higher education, training, professional updating and life-long learning is increasingly to teach the skills of critical thinking, quantitative reasoning and effective communication, along with abilities to find, search, analyse and apply information, and to work well with others in teams. How are institutions re-thinking and redesigning their curricula to address these new teaching and learning requirements? How many faculty and trainers understand the implications of these new demands and are successfully introducing opportunities for their learners to acquire these skills and abilities?

It is my contention, through research on global practice, that it is those educational providers most geared to the international marketplace who are also most attuned to the new function of higher education and training. Communication technology is the means by which they are providing the new curricula and offering the learning opportunities appropriate to the new social order, but the driving force for the best of the global providers is a readiness to respond to students' needs.

Structural changes

One of the characteristics of technology-based education is that it is inherently a team effort. Face-to-face education and training combine seamlessly many aspects of the learning process, which the technology-mediated counterparts tend to de-couple. As soon as the delivery of the course content (for example by CD-ROM, CBT, or Web pages) is separated from the tutorial support to the learner (for example by email, fax, bulletin board), the single lecturer is invariably replaced by a team of technology experts, graphics designers, educational technologists, and course designers, as well as tutors and support services. This team approach often involves a move from decentralised operating units that function independently, to a centralised structure or a network of co-ordinating parts serving the student.

In order to effect change at a structural level, leadership from the top tiers of an organisation are essential. The first act of most vice chancellors or senior management beginning a process of institutional change is to craft a mission statement or at least a policy statement which provides the *raison d'être* for changes to follow. Here is an extract from several such statements:

> Existing universities must assimilate the new communications technologies, and with the utmost effectiveness seek to use the enormous benefits

that the 'digital revolution' promises for the advancement of teaching, learning, research and communications generally. This must be an uncompromising, high priority commitment. Otherwise the traditional university will indeed be threatened with redundancy.

(Gilbert, 1996, p. 4)

The Company seeks to strengthen and expand its position as a provider of knowledge-enhancing programming and distance education products and services to adults. The Company's strategy is: (i) to expand the distribution of its networks, (ii) to license, develop and produce high quality programming for both its networks and degree and certificate courses, (iii) to increase its marketing and promotion activities, (iv) to increase its student enrolments, (v) to develop corporate relationships, (vi) to expand further in international markets, and (vii) to pursue strategic investments, acquisitions and joint ventures.

(Jones Education Company, http://www.jec.edu/))

At the heart of the process must be an aim or, in the new corporate language, a market which the change is being made to address. All the evidence of the global revolution we are undergoing points toward increasing diversity:

- of learners and hence learning types;
- of educational provision (modular courses, specialist courses, postgraduate courses, self-learning materials, mentored courses);
- of educational providers: traditional universities, for-profit universities, corporate universities, and network providers.

In such a context, it is important for an organisation entering the global marketplace to have a clear vision of what it does best, what is to be its core business, and therefore what market it is addressing.

Another move made by a number of 'technology mobile' institutions is to create a new position at a senior level to manage the re-engineering process, called variously director or pro-vice chancellor of technology/virtual/global/distance/knowledge management, depending on the exact emphasis of the institution. Failing this or as part of this new direction, institutions will frequently devise a technology strategy for the organisation, so that all new initiatives, funding and policies can be referred back to a single framework driving the changes (see, for example, Daniel, 1996). Will the strategy encourage innovation through sponsoring a large number of small projects throughout the organisation, or through putting all available monies into a small number of large projects with more visible effects? What aspects of the change-over will be outsourced and what developed in-house? Will all the technology eggs be put in one basket, or will a number of technologies be developed? These are examples of the kinds of questions which such a strategy must address.

Collaborative policies

Almost all of the large applications of global education I have discovered involve collaborative arrangements with other institutions whether in the same country or abroad. The most common partnership is between a content provider and a course presenter. For example, the Jones Education Company works with content providers at half a dozen universities to deliver degree, certificate and vocational courses. Open Learning Agency of Australia commissions courses from participating institutions and all then guarantee credit transfer. The UKOU works with a large number of academic institutions which purchase course materials to present themselves, or to be tutored and accredited by the OU. Other partnerships involve joint preparation of materials or more commonly of programmes made up of courses from participating institutions.

While some collaboration such as this is taking place, most of it is in spite of existing national and local regulations, rather than aided by them. Many of these regulations, or in some cases merely practices which have grown up over time, exist to prevent one organisation poaching the students of another. This competitive approach has frequently been cited as a barrier to the institutional changes needed to respond to the current climate (Granger and Gulliver, 1996). The most obvious example is that of credit transfer – the recognition of courses studied successfully at one institution by another. Needless to say, the difficulties to be overcome in this issue are magnified when applied on a global scale.

In sum, the re-engineered institution does not see itself as an autonomous teaching centre, no matter how large or how prestigious, but as one component in a network reliant on, and strengthened by other organisations performing the same or complementary functions.

Teaching methods

The essence of a changed organisation is teachers and trainers who are genuinely interested in teaching, not just in research or in preserving their jobs. They must be trained in interactive methods which encourage the learner to be actively involved in the material. This may involve moving to self-paced learning and assessment, or to a problem-solving approach rather than narrow discipline-oriented teaching. It will certainly involve moving from lecture-oriented one-way teaching to experiential, interactive learning, and from the teacher as content-provider to the teacher as facilitator and guide. It will probably involve technology – not by simply moving lectures to computer screen or videotape, which merely preserves the status quo – but by re-thinking the curriculum to offer opportunities to master material, provide continual feedback, and to cater for individual learning styles through written, verbal and visual means.

How can intransigent faculty be encouraged to adopt new methods? What sticks or carrots can be used to persuade them to reconsider their current practice? Incentives are particularly difficult to find given that most studies show, and early adopters admit, these new methods generally take more time than traditional approaches.

It is clear from a number of research studies and also from my own investigations that the early adopters of technology-based global education find the intrinsic rewards a major attraction in their participation. The combination of the novelty of the technology, the potential it offers for responding to students' learning needs and the opportunity to expand their horizons beyond the classroom, provide all the incentive they need to dedicate long hours to re-thinking their course, mastering the technology, and interacting with students (see, for example, Taylor, 1996). However, while this may suffice in the short term, it will not build a vibrant teaching faculty in the long term. The primary answer to real re-engineering revolves around a change to the traditional reward and recognition structure of higher education to favour innovation and dedication to teaching rather than to research alone – as study after study continues to make clear (for example, MacFarlane, 1992). Reduction of teaching load or additional monetary rewards for taking on extra students at a distance are also possibilities.

Proper training in the use of new technologies is also essential for all except perhaps the enthusiastic early adopters, and the latter may be appropriate people to at least advise on the nature of the training programme. Thach and Murphy cite a number of examples of technology applications in which the staff received little or no training, and received little recognition and no rewards for their participation (Thach and Murphy, 1996). Consequently the results were not outstanding and in some cases the faculty had reverted to old methods after the initial push. While certain technologies, like videoconferencing and Webcasting, require some adaptation to the technology but little change in teaching strategy, others, like computer conferencing and online courses (where the course consists of Web pages and collaborative online activities), take considerably more 're-engineering' of the whole teaching strategy and hence more training. In my own Institute of Educational Technology, we find the 'apprentice' model most efficacious – new staff 'lurk' for one run of the course (getting a feel for the nature of online courses), then take part as minor tutors for a few presentations (beginning to find their own online style of interaction), before being asked to design and run their own course.

Many train-the-trainer courses exist in all the new technologies, both at the technical level and at the educational level. Some of these are available on the Web (e.g. http://www-iet.open.ac.uk); others are available as text-based self-taught courses (e.g. Barnett *et al.*, 1996). Organisations which are serious about re-engineering will invite educational technologist and training providers to design and run tailor-made programmes for large numbers of their staff.

As with all re-engineering processes, there is something even more important than mission statements, policies, rewards and training, and that is listening to staff concerns and allowing them to participate in deciding the direction and nature of the changes. In fact, as the following description of the process shows, it is not possible to implement 'root and branch' change without the wholehearted support of the people to be changed:

> In beginning to establish a virtual campus we have undertaken an organi-sational change process that has at times created much dissonance and pain. It has required enormous goodwill across the central service sectors and faculties of the University; academic, administrative and information technology staff are experiencing changing job roles, new working rela-tionships and changing structures as they have begun the massive task of supporting students (many of whom are off-campus) and staff across the six campuses . . . all of whom are coming to the technologies with varying levels of computer skills and understandings.
> (Stacey and Thompson, 1996, p. 209)

Staff will be quick to notice when a re-engineering process is initiated for the purposes of 'teaching more for less', rather than for the broader need to re-think the whole system. If maintaining or, better still, improving the quality of the learning experience for students is not a major criterion in the change process, staff will at best be disillusioned, and at worst be resistant. I hope there is evidence in these chapters to support the contention that re-engineering higher education can lead to better teaching and learning.

Technology choices

Part of the re-thinking process will probably involve making choices about which technologies to use to deliver and support students. These choices are never easy, as Ehrmann explains:

> Technological progress is continuous and almost seamless, but capital investment typically takes place in bursts. One must periodically make major investments and then live with the results for a while, improving each year incrementally, until the time comes to make the next big change in hardware. Thus, when it is time to make such a major change in infrastruc-ture, it is tempting to pick the most advanced technology available, something just off the drawing board, perhaps not even in use by industry yet. The temptation increases when vendors, anxious to get a share of the market, offer the experimental technology at a sharp discount or even for 'free'. Such low cost technology is often not so inexpensive in the long run, once the costs of support, maintenance and replacement become manifest.
> (Ehrmann, 1996, p. 34)

It is, as he says, virtually impossible to build powerful new educational programmes by relying on these 'drawing board' technologies. In fact, most evaluation research shows that it is the support structures and the quality of the educational content that matter to learners much more than the technology used to deliver them.

Organisational support structures

While re-engineering a large institution steeped in years of tradition and established practice may be a daunting and lengthy process, there are limits to the impact which single institutions can make in meeting the demands of the new education and training context. Below I outline the work of two organisational support structures which have been formed to help educational providers act on a global level. Many more such organisations will develop as global education expands.

Global Alliance for Transnational Education (GATE)

GATE represents an international alliance of business, higher education and government dedicated to the advocacy of transnational educational programmes. The alliance was founded by Glenn Jones, who is chief executive officer of Jones Education Company (see Chapter 8 for more details). GATE has developed a set of 'Guiding Principles' to assist institutions and organisations in the development and evaluation of quality education which crosses national borders. The principles are adopted by national systems for application to transnational programmes and/or they are applied directly by GATE in a centrally administered international peer review process for quality assurance and improvement, requested on a voluntary basis. The external review leads to GATE recognition which carries with it the professional and moral authority of the international higher education and corporate training communities. One of its key objectives is to protect students from unscrupulous organisations by encouraging providers to seek external certification that they are adhering to internationally agreed guidelines.

The principles cover issues such as standards, student support, pedagogy, financial resources and legal matters. GATE has also drawn up a set of guidelines for institutional recognition as a global educational provider.

The second plank of the GATE alliance is the provision of a global database so that participating organisations have access (both printed and electronic) to national academic standards, quality assurance processes and institutional information (names, affiliations and nature of transnational education entities) in all countries of location. Students, employers and university admissions offices require information about the availability of transnational programmes, the acceptance of such qualifications in their own and other countries and the accredited status of universities across the world. This is obviously an ambitious undertaking and will take time to build up to truly global proportions.

The third mission of GATE is awareness-raising and general communication about issues, trends, and needs of global education. The Web site of GATE goes some way to carrying out this function: http://www.edugate.org – they also hold regular conferences in the form of a global forum.

Higher Education Quality Council (HEQC)

The mission of HEQC is to contribute to the maintenance and improvement of quality in institutions of higher education in the United Kingdom. Because of the growth of collaborative schemes between UK institutions and partners overseas, HEQC has recently extended its national quality auditing procedures to visiting collaborating institutions abroad in order to safeguard quality and standards in overseas provision. In addition, the Council has prepared a code of practice on overseas collaborative provision in higher education, which is regularly updated and revised as further experience is gathered on global education in practice.

The 1996 Report on Quality Assurance of Overseas Partnerships (Stoddart, 1996) is generally reassuring about the standard of UK institutional practice abroad, but warns against complacency and underestimating the potential difficulties of establishing and maintaining high quality provision of education internationally. For example, one of the issues the report tackles is the responsibility of the host institution for the student's total learning experience. It concludes:

> In practice, the evidence from the pilot visits shows that it is difficult for any institution wholly to absolve itself of responsibility for the quality of the students' learning experience without undermining its concern for the standing of its awards, and how that which is done in its name is perceived by others.
>
> (Stoddart, 1996, p. 6)

In short, institutions franchising their courses to partners abroad must ensure that the same provisions are made (for counselling, for checking pre-requisite qualifications, for monitoring assignment and exam standards, for marketing and promoting courses, and for communicating promptly with students) as apply in the host country. This inevitably means that the partnership must be underpinned by formal institutional agreements, outlining the scope, limits and duration of the arrangements. The report noted that:

> Three areas in particular, received either no, or insufficiently detailed, attention in the majority of the written agreements scrutinised by audit teams: quality assurance procedures, including especially mechanisms for securing consistency in assessment practice; rules and requirements for controlling publicity and promotional material and arrangements for identifying residual responsibilities if the partnership ended prematurely, and for safeguarding the interests of the students involved.
>
> (*ibid.*, p. 8)

In those instances where students were assessed through work completed in their own language, the report praised policies which involved the translation of some scripts by independent translators for the purposes of monitoring by the host institution. In addition, it recommended that members of the board of examiners should include individuals with a native command of the local language to act on behalf of the UK awarding institution.

Finally, the report confirmed the common sense response to international partnerships: they cannot be conducted wholly through virtual communication. Physical visits by both senior and working staff must take place at regular intervals to establish good relationships, review procedures, and monitor standards.

Global accreditation

One support structure which is clearly needed for global education to become truly established, is a global accreditation system. Consider the situation of a student taking courses from many different global providers. Who would award the final degree? Currently, universities cling fiercely to their accrediting powers, and national governments continue to play a pre-eminent role in regulating higher education within their national boundaries. A recent report commissioned by the Australian government makes the following recommendations:

> As a matter of urgency, the Federal Government should begin developing legislative frameworks for the certification and accreditation of postsecondary education programs emanating from non-traditional Australian and international institutions and offered electronically or by more traditional means to the general public.
>
> (Cunningham *et al.*, 1997)

It is understandable that countries with small populations want to preserve their indigenous higher education system by raising barriers to global providers. New Zealand, another example, has a total population of about 3.5 million people, served by nine universities and twenty-five polytechnics. There are currently 100 institutions worldwide which have registered New Zealand students. While Indonesia and Malaysia used to supply students to New Zealand universities, increasingly they are turning to bigger named institutions operating globally from the USA and the UK. A global accreditation system might encourage students to take some courses locally and some from global providers.

Steps towards internationalising educational provision

There are certainly many instances of charismatic individuals and even small departments at otherwise 'unregenerated institutions' carrying out really innovative teaching programmes at an international level. They undoubtedly act as 'starter-packs' for their own and even for other institutions. However, it is to those few organisations which have systems and procedures in place at an institutional level to support and manage a teaching programme across several countries that we must turn for models and recommendations about the do's and don'ts of global educational provision. As Daniel points out: 'Today it is the powerful logistics systems required to support large numbers of students nationally and internationally that is harder for campus universities to reproduce' (Daniel, 1996, p. 133).

There are several fledgling organisations which have been set up recently for the specific purpose of providing education on a global scale – the Global Network Academy, and the Global Campus initiative of IBM for example. Others have global intentions from the start but begin primarily at a national level – Jones Education Company and Open Learning Agency of Australia, for example. Finally, there are institutions which have intentionally and progressively moved from being domestic to international providers – the UKOU is a prominent example of this re-engineering. It is instructive to look at issues arising from all three types.

Starting global

The 'green field' global organisations all appear to have a strong telecommunications base to them, whether satellite technology in the case of the Global Network Academy, or computers and the Internet in the case of Global Campus, or interactive computer software in the case of Microsoft's MOLI (Microsoft Online Institute). Partnerships, franchising and collaborations amongst academics are formed in conjunction with the technology to provide the core content. Global access is guaranteed from the start, though the clientele is, at this stage, very specialist. While the strengths of these organisations lie in their freedom from the shackles of historical precedent and in their close ties with the technology for delivering educational material, their weaknesses lie in the accrediting, managing and supporting of courses. On the whole, they tend to be the most innovative in their delivery and conception of learning.

Building global delivery

A large number of educational providers have sprung up in the last five years or so, with their eye firmly fixed on the international market, but which begin by offering distributed or distance education and training on a national level. Some, like Jones Education Company, have already begun to move outside the USA (see Chapter 8) and others are still building up their credentials in the home market. Most of these providers have stronger roots in education or training than those I mentioned in the category above, or have developed strong partnerships with traditional providers. They also tend to be less committed to any one technology for delivery, and 'old fashioned' print still plays a role in the programme. These providers have systems for accrediting and administering courses, and many have adopted innovative approaches to the curriculum and to its delivery. As national providers, they are growing in strength and beginning to compete with traditional institutions. They tend to be weak in their approaches to building global alliances.

Re-engineering globally

A small number of universities – either distance teaching institutions or the new virtual universities – have begun a process of re-engineering which has led them to a new or much enhanced global strategy for growth and development. From an examination of their processes and systems for operating globally, I have compiled the following checklist of elements which must be considered in providing courses for students outside the host country:

Courses and awards to be offered

The first consideration is the decision about which courses or full programmes to offer, and in which countries. How much adaptation will be carried out and by whom? On existing material, copyright clearance must be obtained for all countries in the global programme. The most significant cultural, linguistic and pedagogical differences of the students in the target country need to be identified and brought to bear on the proposed content, particularly the assignment and exam questions.

Administering student entry

This process begins with the marketing of the course(s). A wide range of promotion techniques will need to be considered and adapted to the local context. Once interest has been engaged it is necessary to offer advice to inquirers so that they can make an informed choice and register for it. The methods of delivering advice will vary in each market – brochures, telephone, the Web, listservs on the Internet, local centres – all may be necessary but the common element is accurate information delivered by skilled and trained staff.

A system of record keeping with a means of identifying each student in the database is essential. In some cases credentials (such as language proficiency or previous degrees) will have to be checked. Certain restrictions or rules operating in the host country may not be legal in another. (For example, in the UK the OU imposes a lower age limit of 27 on those entering its MBA programme. This is not legal in the USA).

In setting and collecting fees from students, the institution should not simply make a conversion into local currency of the fee charged in the host country. Adjustments for the cost of living, the competition and the target population will need to be taken into consideration. Billing arrangements will also vary according to country, and payment options will have to be aligned to the legal and cultural context of each country. (Consider, for example, the question of local sales taxes, mail order legislation, attitudes to credit.) Credit referencing will also need to be handled in order to reduce the risk of bad debt. Public and private student financing and bursary schemes will need to be understood and marketed.

Delivery of the course

The course contents will need to be prepared for delivery in good time. In the case of physical components such as print, video and audio cassettes, they will need to be collected and readied for dispatch through a system appropriate for the target country (the regular post, private postal systems, collection by the student from local centres). Clearing customs of such items is not always straightforward.

Virtual course components delivered via the Internet, the telephone, broadcasting or satellite place different demands, but one thing they all have in common is the need for technical support, whether in the form of local staff on site, or remote help desk facilities.

Teachers or tutors to interact with students will need to be hired or designated. If these are to come from the target country, qualifications and experience will have to be specified and contracts of employment drawn up in accordance with local laws. Processes need to be put in place to train the tutors and other locally recruited staff.

As we have seen from the HEQC, the host institution retains some responsibility for the advising and counselling of the students in the target country, even when a local educational institution is involved in the course delivery. Arrangements for this, and for clear demarcations between the responsibilities of the host and those of the local institution, are necessary.

Monitoring the quality of the programme

The host institution will require systems for monitoring the teaching or tutoring of the course(s), and on-site visits to the target country will be a necessary part of this process as well as of the general assurance of quality provision to students. Other mechanisms may include monitoring of tutors' marking of assignments at regular intervals. In addition, evaluation studies of the whole programme should be undertaken to include feedback from students, on-site staff and teachers or tutors.

Assessing students

Systems will have to be put in place for collecting and marking tests and assignments given throughout the course(s), and for recording the results. Final examination arrangements will need careful timetabling, taking into account time zones around the world. If the exam is to be carried out under controlled conditions, arrangements will be needed for proctoring as well as for delivering the paper securely to many sites, and collecting the students' scripts.

Finally, once students have completed their courses and final grades determined, there are certification processes to be established. These may range from simply notifying results through the posting of formal certificates, to arrangements for local graduation ceremonies.

Table 5.1 shows this list in tabular form. Complex as it is, it still does not really cover the intricacies of joint course development or the details of establishing local partnerships. Both of these add yet further steps to the process.

Conclusions

My arguments in this chapter have centred on the need for the re-engineering of the institution – the re-thinking of all its teaching and learning processes in the light of changing pressures and demands – to drive both the entry into global markets and the choice of technologies to support any changes.

I have suggested a number of means by which various universities are currently managing the change process, and have tried to emphasise the importance of involving staff by providing opportunities for them to voice their concerns and be proactive rather than merely reactive to the re-engineering process.

The need for institutional partnerships is critical to any significant move onto the global scene. The complexities of operating in a number of countries are simply too great, as my listing of the major components of a global distance education system shows. Universities have never been notable for their excellence in inter-institutional collaboration – at least not in teaching collaboratively. Quite the contrary. Learning how to do this successfully at an international level will be a significant component of the re-engineering process.

Table 5.1 Organisational issues

Courses	Marketing	Delivery	Monitoring	Assessing
Adaptation	Registering	Technology • access • support • customs	Tutors	Proctoring arrangements
Rights clearance	Credentials	Materials	Assignments	Collecting/ marking
Versioning materials	Fees	Hiring tutors • training Advising Counselling	Evaluate courses	Timetabling Graduating

Part II

Applications of global education

Methodology

In the preceding chapters, I have discussed a wide range of fundamental concerns about the growing trend towards global education, including cultural, pedagogical, and institutional issues. I now turn to an examination of actual practice and consider five examples of what I deem to be a cross section of current activity in higher education and training operating globally.

My choice of courses to investigate was based on the following criteria:

- each course must fulfil at least two of my definitions of a global course (see Chapter 1);
- the overall selection should represent a range of technologies for delivering global courses, a range of countries and types of institution originating the course, a range of curriculum areas, and a range of sectors (undergraduate, graduate, professional, training).

My evaluation methodology consisted of drawing up a list of focus points and questions, derived from the issues raised in the first section of the book. I used this list in gathering data from the major actors on each course. My investigations involved interviewing deans and directors, course designers and tutors or teachers, institutional support staff and, most importantly, students. Interviews were carried out face-to-face, by telephone and by email. Although there is no intention of comparing the courses one to another, I have used a similar framework in presenting the data for each course. I hope this will help the reader to reconsider the issues of globalisation raised earlier, in the light of evidence from practical applications.

Overview of case studies

1 Global Executive MBA, Duke University, USA (Chapter 6).
2 Diploma in Open Learning, University of Southern Queensland, Australia (Chapter 7).
3 Jones Education Company: Knowledge TV and College Connection (Chapter 8).

4   IBM Global Campus (Chapter 9).
5   The UK Open University (Chapter 10).

6   Global Executive MBA, Duke University, North Carolina

Origins of the course

Several 'early adopters' of new technology and distance education on the staff of the Fuqua School of Business at Duke University proposed the notion of a global course using telecommunications technologies, and began to sell the idea to their colleagues in the school. By May 1995, a decision had been made to begin preparing the course for presentation in June 1996, and Dr Rick Staelin took on the directorship of the programme. Intensive discussion began amongst the group of staff who agreed to teach on the course: seven of the fifteen staff were chair professors whose primary interest in the course was its innovative approach and use of technology.

By September a brochure describing the course had been produced and sent to alumni, and Dr Staelin and others began a promotional campaign visiting 160 firms around the world (Korea, Malaysia, Brazil, etc.) to interest them in sponsoring members of their staff to take this global MBA. By December, ten applications had been received. Dr Staelin then prepared an advertisement for *The Economist*, *Financial Times*, *Business Week* and several journals in South America and Asia (see Figure 6.1). Associated with this was a Web site giving more details and explaining the global focus of the programme. Three thousand inquiries were received! Dr Staelin commented:

> We were surprised at the extent of the demand. Through the ad, we tapped an unexpected market – entrepreneurs and heads of small companies. Many people wanted to take the course to change careers or at least to extend their possibilities.
>
> (Personal communication)

Having aimed for twenty-five students, they found themselves with forty-five by the start of the course. Three of these had to drop out due primarily to pressure of work, but the original student profile was as follows:

- twenty-two Americans;

IMAGINE ATTENDING THE WORLD'S LEADING GLOBAL MBA PROGRAM

...without having to relocate or stop working. Travel around the world, communicate through interactive technologies and prepare yourself to lead a global corporation into the 21st century. Duke University's Fuqua School of Business offers an unparalleled educational experience—the Global Executive MBA (GEMBA™) program. The next class begins in May 1997.

 ON LINE Interact with world-class faculty and a select group of students from all parts of the globe. Use the World Wide Web, electronic bulletin boards, e-mail, computer-based video conferencing, asynchronous groupware, decision support software, CD-ROM, multimedia courseware, chatware and more.

 ON SITE Spend 11 weeks in residential classes at locations around the world. At each of five program sites, study local conditions of the region. Learn firsthand how to succeed in a truly global enterprise. Begin with orientation at the Duke campus in North America. Then return to your job and continue interacting and learning via the Internet. Reconvene for two-week sessions in September 1997 in Salzburg, February 1998 in Shanghai, and June 1998 in São Paulo. Return to Duke in November 1998 for the final module of this exciting 19-month Global Executive MBA program.

 ON TARGET Earn your MBA in the only program to fully integrate three essential elements for effective global management: a firm grasp of core business skills, expertise in global management and proficiency in the latest interactive communications technologies. In 15 courses, cover core business functions such as finance, marketing, accounting and decision sciences, as well as the current realities of global business.

 ON TIME Prepare yourself for leadership in a global corporation of the 21st century. Applications close February 1, 1997. Last year's class was oversubscribed, so apply now. For information on GEMBA and Fuqua's other executive programs, contact us today:

Call 919-660-8011 or 800-372-3932 (U.S.)
Fax 919-660-8044
fuqua-execed@mail.duke.edu
http://www.fuqua.duke.edu/programs/gemba

OFFICE IN BRUSSELS

DUKE
THE FUQUA SCHOOL OF BUSINESS

FUQUA. SHAPING BUSINESS REALITIES WORLDWIDE

Figure 6.1 GEMBA's first advertisement

- twenty-three non-Americans, of which eight or nine are expatriate Americans now living abroad.

About 15 per cent are female and about 15 per cent are paying their own fees. All of them are in full-time employment; most are senior managers and some are owners of small businesses. The average age is 39. Apart from Americans, the students come from Japan, Korea, Mexico, Brazil, Poland, Switzerland, the UK and Hong Kong. This quite definitely fulfils the first criterion of a global course: a global student body!

Structure of the course

The course lasts for nineteen months and consists of three parts: short pre-assignment reading periods, five residential meetings of two to three weeks and, in between, a distance education part delivered with a combination of media on the Web. As a component of the course fee, students are each provided with an IBM ThinkPad portable PC. This machine includes a CD-ROM and modem, both of which are integral features of the distance education aspect of the course.

Course content

'International MBAs' offered by other institutions concentrate on issues of how large multinationals do business. By contrast, the Global Executive MBA, called GEMBA, is based on a traditional MBA curriculum but builds into this a global perspective, such as how business is carried out in a range of countries and what works in different cultures. Dr Staelin said that although the course was based on their face-to-face MBA, essentially they 'started with a blank piece of paper'. Because the students of GEMBA were older, more diverse, and working managers rather than young students, the course was designed to be less about business techniques and more about managerial implications. For example, the subject of cash flow analysis concentrates less on 'how to do it' and more on 'how to interpret it'. Some of the fifteen parts of the course have no parallel in the Fuqua School day time MBA programme.

> They learn the core functional areas of business, as well as how to integrate them and how to think and manage globally. . . . All courses have an international theme woven through course topics, assignments and class discussions.
>
> (http://www.fuqua.duke.edu/programs/gemba)

One of the major components of the course is the emphasis on collaborative work amongst the students. To this end, students are divided into eight small group teams and throughout the course of the programme, members will be moved around at least twice so that everyone has the opportunity of working with a range of other students. While some of the course assignments are individual, many require a team approach and are given a team mark. Students are encouraged to regard others in their group as their first source of support for questions, discussion and queries about the course.

Technology support

Running through the whole nineteen months and providing the backbone for the course is the Web site, providing an innovative mix of multimedia technologies for delivering course content and supporting discussion. RealAudio software is used to insert informal 'fireside chats' by the professor about particular topics which enliven the text-based material, or to provide a short interview with a guest 'lecturer' as a way of introducing him or her to the students, or to give general comments about assignments. Screen Cam movies, read off the CD-ROM, are also used to talk students through a spread sheet exercise or other piece of software. Figure 6.2 illustrates a page from the Web site associated with the course.

The bulletin board system which supports the discussion and team work is based on Web frames: one frame shows the list of conferences; another shows the list of messages within a selected conference (including the links between one message and another); and the third frame displays the message selected. This system provides very easy reference and insurance against the 'lost-in cyberspace' feeling so common in Internet messaging. GEMBA uses a range of conferences (or boards, as they refer to them) including a plenary area, a lounge, and a staff-only area, and each team has its own password-protected board for group work. Real time chat facilities had been provided on a trial basis during the first term of the course, and had proven successful enough to be added to the list of core technologies for the course. A videophone system for intra-group discussion was about to be given a similar test to see whether students would find it useful as a support tool.

Between 40 and 50 per cent of the course content is delivered through the face-to-face lectures at the five residential meetings. The other 50 to 60 per cent is delivered through readings and Web-based materials and activities.

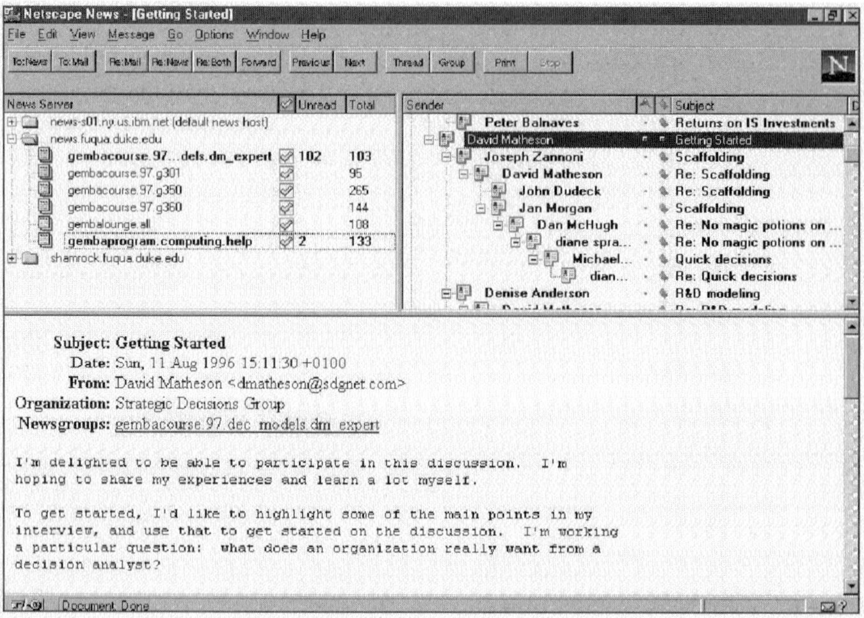

Figure 6.2 Web conferencing on GEMBA

However, staff reckon that nearly half of the 'learning' of the course takes place in the online discussions and collaborative group activities.

Evaluation data

I arrived in Salzburg for the second of the residential components of the course. (The next meeting would be in Shanghai, followed by São Paulo and finally North Carolina.) One of the classes I attended with the students was actually student-initiated. An expatriate American living in Japan encouraged two Japanese colleagues on the course to give a demonstration of the process of introduction, seating, card exchange and conduct of business in that culture. This led to discussion about how foreigners should conduct themselves in relation to these formal aspects of doing business in Japan. This was followed by a similar role play between two Polish students on the course. Requests were made by the students for further sessions of this sort at later residential meetings. This was a very lively session with comments and questions from many of the participants, and it was pointed out to me later that it was the first 'presentation' by one of the Japanese students, whose confidence and command of English had improved markedly since the beginning of the course five months earlier.

Another more traditional class I attended was dominated by American and English mother tongue students, and the lecturer used American jargon and examples (of bowling alleys and shoe rental) which it is doubtful that the non-Americans would follow.

These two classes seem to reflect the basic reality of the course: that it is avowedly an American MBA, but it aims to provide a global perspective on management issues. It has a traditional approach to course content, yet it is responsive to students' needs and requests.

Student feedback

I spoke with at least a dozen students on the course, asking them a range of questions about the collaborative activities, the technology support, cultural issues, the global perspective and what they were gaining from the course. The overall feedback was immensely positive: the high quality of the course content, its relevance to their day job, the unique global perspective, the contribution of other students on the course, and the use of the technology in fostering a learning environment despite distance.

All of the students I questioned had chosen the course specifically because of its global perspective. 'My company expects me to begin managing a major overseas programme shortly and this course is giving me exactly the background I need,' said one student, and others commented on the value of interacting with staff and students who are globally minded. They welcomed the opportunity of developing close friendships with people in countries which they might some day be visiting on business: 'When I go to Korea, the first thing I will do is contact [K].' Students referred to the online discussions in which people would jump in with comments like, 'Oh no, that won't work over here.' This diversity of explanation and detail of how to manage in other cultures was definitely one of the main successes of the course.

Another contributing factor to the global perspective of the course are the residential meetings in different parts of the world. Furthermore, at each of these meetings local business managers are invited to give guest lectures, although apparently these had not been very successful at the first meeting. However, the speaker chosen for the Salzburg meeting had been far more relevant to the students' concerns. One of the students commented to me that generally the expertise of the faculty was limited by their academic rather than practical background. The guest speaker programme was one way of making up for this shortcoming.

I asked some of the non-American students whether they felt that this course was contributing to the Americanisation of global culture or the undermining of indigenous courses. This perspective clearly did not accord with their experience. One student responded: 'I know the Korean way and now I am learning the American way.' His fellow students said that he was becoming more active in contributing to online discussions and speaking up in his small group. Another student said that she wasn't concerned about it being an American degree – she chose it because of the global content. If it had been offered by a British or European institution, she would have taken that.

The telecommunications technology used on the course proved to be as much the subject of the course as the original designers intended: 'As students gain experience in the use of information technology, they develop an understanding of how this technology can and should be used to manage global organizations' (http://www.fuqua.duke.edu/programs/gemba).

A number of students commented on the spin-off in their own business of the communications technologies used on the course.

> We are trying things out on the course which I am wrestling with at work – like how much face-to-face negotiation is necessary in business and how much can be conducted through text-based interaction. What content is carried in text, and what is the role of meetings?

Several students commented on how surprisingly personal text-based interaction was. 'It is as good as class discussion,' some said, but others preferred visual clues and were keen to try out the videoconferencing software to be introduced in the next module. A number had introduced electronic communication into their workplace based on their experience on the course.

I asked about logging on difficulties from various parts of the world. Undoubtedly there had been a few problems with this aspect of the technology, but primarily from students travelling on business and trying to log in from hotel rooms. Some had resorted to making long distance calls rather than attempting to negotiate local Internet providers.

All of the students mentioned the need to develop their ability to manage their time effectively in taking this course on top of family and job commitments. Many discussed the arrangements they had made with colleagues and family in order to undertake the course: for example, fixed times for study in exchange for other times being family time; devolving responsibilities and tasks to colleagues in exchange for pull through to colleagues about course content. Students described the workload of the course as being 'like drinking from a fire hose'. The bonding and support from other students on the course, which developed on the text-based conferencing system and was reinforced at the face-to-face meetings, clearly provided the significant motivational impetus for the course. The students talked about how much they had changed since beginning the course. Their discussion of this focused on the effects of having to prioritise all their activities, and in some cases this had had positive benefits – in their relationships with family and colleagues and in their greater efficiency and effectiveness at work.

I was interested in the reaction of those students operating in their second language to the use of the technology and to the sensitivities of other students and faculty. One Japanese speaker confirmed the general finding about asynchronous text-based interaction systems for foreign language users: 'The virtual classroom is a substantial advantage for foreign students with language difficulties. I can work at my own pace and go back to a classmate's comments if I don't understand them at once' (http://www.fuqua.duke.edu/programs/gemba).

Another oriental student said that he was given extra time to complete the exam at the end of the first term. All students had taken this at a distance and submitted it electronically.

At this point in the course (one quarter of the way through), it is perhaps not surprising that students were uniformly enthusiastic; nevertheless, it does seem that the global focus of this course is meeting a definite need in the market and the technology to deliver it is contributing positively to the learning environment.

Faculty views

My discussions with various faculty members teaching on the programme centred on the issues of quality in a technology-mediated and globally dispersed teaching cnvironmcnt. I also asked about the curriculum and the extent to which it had been changed to meet the demands of a global student body. 'What do you do about a student who says that he doesn't need to know statistics in his job and would like to omit this part of the course?' I asked. The response was unequivocal:

> While we try to be responsive, the primary consideration is that this MBA stands for a set of core skills, competencies and knowledge. We want employers to know there are things they can count on from a Duke

MBA. The explosion of MBA courses during the 1970s has led to a greater distinction being made now about which institution has granted the degree.

I also asked faculty members about their views on the approach taken by some educational providers, that students and employers are consumers whose demands for course content of a particular type, length and appropriateness, needed to be met and that the curriculum of many academic-driven courses was too theoretical, out-of-date and unrelated to real-world problems. The stance taken by the GEMBA faculty lies closer to 'academic ivory tower traditionalism' than to popular 'consumerism'. 'I'd be very worried about a consumer mentality coming into Duke'. Nevertheless, the faculty spent considerable time and effort on three elements often associated with consumer-led programmes:

Responsiveness to feedback from students

Staff read and contributed to the online discussions, took many informal opportunities to talk with students at the residential meetings and raised any significant issues with their fellow members of staff for discussion and resolution. For example, they decided after long debates as a team, to take a hard line on completion deadlines for work from students. 'We felt it was important that students start each new term with a fresh slate – not with unfinished work from the previous term.' Nevertheless, they extended the regular completion day for work to be submitted from Friday to Monday, in response to students' comments that the weekend was often their best time for uninterrupted study.

Leading edge use of technology

An important part of the course is the use of multimedia technologies for delivering the half of the course which is non-residential. In addition to the relatively common technologies of Web browsers, application sharing, CD-ROM, email, streaming audio and computer conferencing (both synchronous and asynchronous), the faculty are experimenting with computer-based videoconferencing, streaming video and voice-over-network synchronous discussions. The use of these technologies has been a major challenge for the faculty, and some have responded more enthusiastically than others. However, the early success of the technology in the first term has led to a greater desire to experiment and to refine the use of some of the first trials. One professor admitted that he had been proved wrong and that he had come to see that the technology was actually a positive element of the course.

Up-to-date course content

The technology used on the course permitted faculty to 'work on the fly' to revise the course content (e.g. by recording RealAudio mini lectures and Screen Cam explanations) and to introduce discussions on the conferencing system to help students having particular difficulties or to enlarge on areas which were particularly interesting. One student said, 'It is critical to me that this course is up-to-date.' Faculty used a combination of experimentation, close communication with students and faculty consultation to maintain its leading edge position. One member of staff pointed out that Duke University is a private institution and on the whole they were much faster at responding to changes in the external environment than were the large state universities.

The GEMBA programme represents an innovative step for Duke University in a number of ways: the content, the use of technology and the distance education part of the course. Together these implied another change to traditional practice: this was the first programme to use a team approach to course design. The fifteen faculty teaching the course attend meetings to plan the course content, to decide on common approaches and to consider problems as they arise on the course. This is quite a different paradigm from the usual individual professor as 'king in his classroom'. One decision made from the outset of the programme was that teaching on this course resulted in double the workload credit for each faculty member compared with face-to-face teaching. As the director said, 'We've thrown a lot of resources at this course!'

I asked the staff what provisions they made to maintain quality and to set high standards of teaching on the course. One of the practices they had instituted was attending each other's lectures at the residential meetings, and as mentioned above, they held regular meetings as a team to discuss course issues and report any difficulties. From the technical support staff, they were regularly up-dated with log-on statistics, and any student not contributing to the online discussions was telephoned after about ten days. 'We know that things come up – at home or on the job. . . . Sometimes all the staff will consider how to get the student re-engaged.' However, the most important element in keeping in touch with how the course was progressing was undoubtedly the conferences and personal email. 'Students on this course are very vocal. We know immediately when things aren't going well.'

The innovative nature of the course did mean that some aspects of the provision would not be successful. 'We are all learning from the failures.' In the first term, faculty were really exploring the technology, trying to see which parts of the curriculum could be delivered with which media. 'Sometimes this was too innovatory, done too much on the fly and it showed.' While they expected to be able to re-use much of the course materials for the next presentation of the course, the least successful parts would be re-made. 'We are aiming to become the premiere global MBA available.'

One faculty member commented to me that she saw future competition for this type of course coming from Asian universities such as those in Singapore, where many of the staff had top degrees from prestigious institutions in the West.

Institutional considerations

The ways in which the institution had adapted to the demands of supporting and resourcing this global course were my primary considerations in talking with support staff. In addition to administrative and clerical staff, the programme had a full time technical support person who set up the students' machines, provided updates of software at each residential meeting, gathered computer-generated statistics for the faculty, maintained the Web site, answered technical queries, and helped students with telecommunications access difficulties. Another software expert contributed half time to the programme in setting up the computer environment, selecting the core software and investigating new experimental media.

I inquired about provisions for accessing the Web with such a dispersed student body. The technical support member of staff assigned to the course full time explained that each student made their own arrangements with a local Internet provider before the course began. She then configured each individual's machine to provide automatic log-on. Although access to the Web had presented difficulties for some students during the first term, most of the problems had now been resolved. She also said that, in order to reduce the load for remote students, graphics were used sparingly on the Web pages. For example, a digitised photo of each student is attached to their personal details because it is so valuable in adding telepresence to the group and in helping students to get to know each other. Pictures of social occasions at the previous residential meeting were available on the Web site as well as maps and photos of Salzburg, but all of these were optional. Despite these and other provisions for students accessing from remote locations, many of the students 'spent most of the first term just getting up to speed with the technology'.

The GEMBA programme includes another unique feature. Prompted by the innovative nature of the course – in terms of the global reach and the use of communications technologies – the director instigated a learning partnership contract to which everyone on the course gives allegiance at the start. An extract from this agreement is reproduced below. Similar contracts have been drawn up for other virtual courses (Mason, 1993), but this one reflects the kind of cultural and attitudinal sensitivities that are bound to arise on a global course. The responsibilities of students to make the course a success are also notable.

Extract from the Fuqua learning partnership

The mission of the Fuqua School of Business (FSB) is to enhance the practice of management through research and teaching. FSB recognizes that the ability and willingness to teach and learn reside in the individual. If very high levels of knowledge transfer are to occur, it is necessary for all members of the FSB community to understand and respect their mutual obligations. The learning partnership can be defined as:

- Respect for individual differences: the Fuqua School values the strengths which result from its diverse community. Each person brings a unique set of experiences and thus a unique perspective to each interaction. If all parties are open to empathic understanding of issues from a myriad of perspectives, learning can flourish.
- Respect for the intellectual environment: the Fuqua School's learning environment is characterized by teamwork, collaboration, and support. Learning is not a unidirectional activity; both students and faculty must commit to active participation in the process. Everyone should remain attentive to the speaker; practice courtesy in personal interactions; understand the need for flexibility; and take personal responsibility for choices and actions.
- A strong, personal commitment to honesty, excellence, and intellectual propriety: academic institutions thrive on personal honor and integrity. To help define accepted standards of conduct, the FSB community has created and refined an honor code to govern actions in the classroom and promote a community spirit of trust, respect, and personal integrity.
- An openness to the risks inherent in the pursuit of knowledge: the quest for knowledge requires a certain vulnerability. Students must open themselves to new ideas and new perspectives, some of which may threaten beliefs which have been closely held. In their quest to improve the educational process, faculty may try new approaches to teaching. Remaining open to new ways of thinking and new ways of doing allows the transfer of knowledge to occur.

Operationalizing the learning partnership

Achieving the above ideals requires mutual commitment to specific behavioral principles, some of which are outlined below:

- Elements of the student role in the learning partnership include: treating the classroom as a professional responsibility; arriving on time and fully prepared for each class; communicating ideas and opinions in a way which demonstrates respect for others; taking responsibility for the successful transfer of knowledge; providing objective and constructive feedback through appropriate channels; understanding that the honor code remains in effect at all times and asking for clarification about any aspect of the code which is unclear prior to commencing assigned work.
- Elements of the faculty role in the learning partnership include: treating the classroom as a professional experience; starting class on time and being fully prepared; communicating ideas and opinions in a way

which reflects awareness of others' views; challenging students to think in new and different ways; providing honest and constructive feedback to enhance student learning; explicitly stating any specific ways that the honor code applies to the course; and answering students' questions about application of the code in completing assignments.

If consistently adhered to by all FSB community members these basic standards will ensure a high quality educational experience for all. Beyond the FSB community, these elements will add value to the Fuqua MBA degree and enrich each member's personal and professional life.

I asked the director about the impact of this course on the rest of the institution. Due to the success of the Web-based media in providing an environment for collaboration, friendship and interactive discussion, the technology had already been extended to the face-to-face MBA programme. It was clear from the numbers of students attracted to the first presentation of the course that a new market had been tapped by the concept and design of the course. The current plan was to allow the programme to expand to about double the present number of students.

One very important institutional issue came up in discussion with faculty staff: the extent to which this kind of technology-mediated course required teachers to become producers and educational technologists: 'We have to think about how to convey content, to consider which medium is best for each aspect of the course material. This is an incredible challenge.' The director was convinced that the success of the course lay in the use of technologies which did not require huge sunk costs in technology. 'We've got to be able to work on the fly without media experts. We want an informal approach with technologies that allow experimentation.' Certainly the examples I was shown (of RealAudio clips and Screen Cam presentations) had all the best features of this kind of use of technology: they conveyed a real sense of the presence of the lecturer; they were engaging in their informality and stimulating in the immediacy of the content they conveyed.

Analysis and conclusions

What lessons can we learn from this example of global education? What conclusions can we draw about the practice of global education from this case study? My analysis covers the following four areas: the global benefits achieved by the course; the technology strategy underpinning the course; the pedagogical direction, and the institutional impact.

Benefits from global perspective

The first thing to note about this course is that the global aspect has not been 'bolted on' to an otherwise existing course. On the contrary, it has been built into the whole conception of the course. Every module of the course has been re-conceived with a global perspective in mind. Second, the resources dedicated to marketing the course on a global scale have made a significant contribution to the truly global spread of the first student body. This is not 'token globalism' but globalisation by design. Third, and most importantly, the nature of the course lends itself more appropriately to a global perspective than probably any other single area of the tertiary education and training curriculum. It is easy to conclude that the Global Executive MBA is a concept whose time had come. The benefits to GEMBA students of both the global perspective of the content and the global reach of the student body, are indisputable. Either element on its own (a global perspective but a national student body, or a global student body with a completely traditional content) would have been much inferior. What we see in this programme is the bench mark to which any other global course designers should aspire.

Technology strategy

It is significant that only half of the course content is delivered 'virtually', and that extended face-to-face periods are available to overcome any pedagogical, social and technical problems. The use of a single student machine configured by central staff overcomes many potential technical problems. The generous staff/student ratio, the workload reduction which allows staff to dedicate double the time to this course, and the relatively small numbers of students overall mean that each student receives a considerable amount of personal care and attention, both online and face-to-face. This course is clearly 'top of the range'. The fees are very high and the input of resources is commensurate with this: the hardware, resources and staff (both quantity and quality).

Nevertheless, there are lessons to learn from the technology strategy of this course even for practitioners aiming for a different market. The first is that the media have all been integrated into the single framework of the Web: audio elements are linked seamlessly to the Web pages; discussion areas are a click away; core software is all incorporated into one interface. Second, the 'ownership' of the course content by the teaching faculty through the use of 'low tech' solutions which allow material to be produced informally (e.g. recordings made on audiotapes at home) and easily revised, contributes to a dynamic, innovatory and committed approach to the technology. Third, the input of an enthusiastic and knowledgeable Web expert providing technical and design support from the beginning has underpinned the success of the virtual environment.

Pedagogical transformation

To what extent has the technology and the global scope of the course led to a transformation of the teaching strategy of the course? The emphasis on group work and learning from peers through the use of team affiliations and team marks for assignments is a cornerstone of the programme. It signals a move away from a teacher-led pedagogy and is an approach which has developed hand-in-hand with the availability of text-based interactive communications technology. The course team approach of the teaching staff is also a move away from standard practice at Duke. The innovative use of technology and the global scope of the course were the main attractions to the faculty who chose to involve themselves with the programme.

Nevertheless, the emphasis on quality and traditional MBA standards has characterised this programme much more pervasively than real experimentation with the curriculum. Aspects of other global and virtual courses taught elsewhere, such as choice amongst a range of modules to make up a degree, rolling intake, emphasis on practical rather than theoretical approaches, social construction of knowledge, etc. have not figured in this application. The result is a course whose quality can be assessed by all the standard procedures and whose workload can be measured by traditional means.

Institutional change

It is early days to look for signs of institutional change from a programme as new as this. The Fuqua School of Business has had a policy of attracting foreign students to its campus-based MBA for some time. In fact, an office in Brussels is maintained for directing and administering this policy. The director of GEMBA imagines the programme doubling in size for the next presentation and inevitably this will have institutional implications. But the desire to avoid setting up an infrastructure of media experts and relying on technology solutions beyond the scope of faculty to manage themselves, means that the programme can continue to run with little impact on the normal structure of a face-to-face campus-based institution.

7 Graduate Certificate in Open and Distance Learning, USQ

Origins of the programme

A Graduate Certificate in Open and Distance Learning has been developed as a series of Web-based courses by the University of Southern Queensland (USQ) in Australia. The programme is aimed at academic and training personnel who want to improve their knowledge and skill in the design, delivery and management of open and distance learning. During 1996, the first two courses were prepared and delivered to a pilot group of students. During 1997, more courses were added, including one on creating interactive multimedia, and about seven other courses are now being developed in order to offer a choice of credit points to make up the Certificate.

USQ already has considerable credentials as a distance teaching institution: it has been involved in distance education since 1977 and currently has more than 16,000 students enrolled from all over Australia. Furthermore, it has a strong tradition of international provision of education: about 20 per cent of its on-campus students are foreign and between 2,000 and 3,000 students actually study at a distance from countries such as Kuala Lumpur, Singapore, Hong Kong and Malaysia. In fact, the university has established a number of offices abroad, for instance in Indonesia, the Philippines, Korea and the United Arab Emirates. While the instructional materials for most courses are primarily print-based, audiotapes, videotapes and computer-managed learning packages are also used. Student support is offered through local study centres staffed by regional liaison officers, as well as by telephone and email contact with the Distance Education Centre at the main campus in Toowoomba, Queensland. Tutorials are provided in a range of ways: face-to-face (and in the case of Hong Kong and Malaysia, staff fly out for a week at a time), audioconferencing, and occasionally audiographics (although the latter two are not yet offered internationally).

Therefore, while the use of the Web as the primary delivery medium for the Certificate represented a new departure for USQ, it was built upon considerable experience and infrastructure in delivering courses internationally.

The initiative has been funded by grants from the Australian Federal Government and a Global Learning Initiative of AT&T and the International

Council for Distance Education (ICDE). For the initial pilot version, ten collaborating institutions worldwide agreed to put forward several members of staff to take the 1996 courses. Subsequent participants in the programme will be fee-paying.

In all, twenty-two students signed up for the first course on 'Designing Instruction for Open and Distance Learning'. All of them were members of staff from educational institutions in the US, Malaysia, Mexico, South Africa, Brunei, Canada, and the Solomon Islands.

Structure of the course

Courses within the programme consist of tailor-made Web pages, interaction through a Web conferencing system and recommended readings. These readings (book chapters and articles) were not provided by USQ; as students were members of an academic institution, it was assumed that they could acquire the books and journals through normal library procedures. While the number of recommended readings varies from course to course (a list of the readings for each course is available at http://www.usq.edu.au/material/course/US59), as do the number of Web pages associated with each course, it is probably more accurate to say that the bulk of the content of the course is actually in the readings, with the Web materials offering a framework and guide to the subject.

The programme has been developed by a team of academics and support staff from the Distance Education Centre, the Department of Further Education and Training, Media Services, IT services and the Library. They have had regular meetings to co-ordinate the programme and to consider a range of issues in supporting Web-based courses. However, on the whole, the Web content of each course is written and tutored by an individual academic.

Each topic in the course, Instructional Design Architectures, follows the same pattern: experiencing, reflecting, conceptualising and applying the learned concepts (Naidu, 1997). First the student studies the material provided on the Web and follows up the Web references. After reflecting on the ideas, they enter the conceptualisation phase through interaction online with the tutor and other students. The final stage of applying the concepts takes place in the formal assessment work.

One member of staff was hired specifically to support the course: a library assistant whose task was to search the Internet for relevant support materials for the courses. The results of this search revealed

> thirty-one electronic journals and magazines and 43 newsletters relevant to educational technology, as well as 12 electronic journals related to distance education, 29 electronic journals related to instructional technology, 28 associated electronic discussion groups and numerous databases all specifically related to the content of the course.
>
> (Taylor and Swannell, 1997)

It is obvious why courses about distance education, technology-based education and course design, are one of the most common subjects for global courses – so much of the content for such courses is already available from the Web! After 150 hours the resulting list of Web sites and Internet documents was co-ordinated into the programme 'Treasure Trove', shown in Figure 7.1. The materials are not only related to the appropriate course, but they are annotated to allow the student to make some judgement about their usefulness before connecting to them. In addition to this prepared list of references and links, the library offers a Virtual Reference Desk, as they explain in the course support materials:

> This service has been designed to support courses that USQ offers electronically over the Internet. We can't send you print materials. However, we are able to assist you to search the Internet for electronic materials, and can give you advice about searching of databases for both print- and electronic resources. You'll receive an answer via e-mail, usually within twenty-four hours.

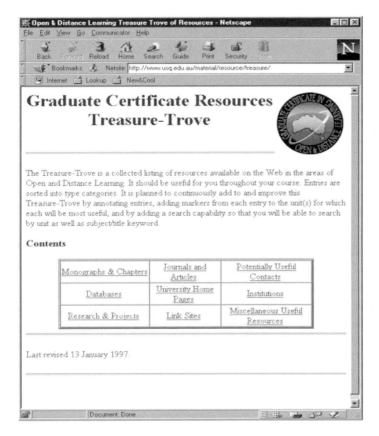

Figure 7.1 The Treasure Trove Web page

Another document about Web navigation and communication was prepared by a member of the Distance Education Centre support staff. As a general introduction to Web use, it acts as an online guide for students on all of the courses about aspects of the Web they will need to understand in order to study the courses. The homepage of the Graduate Certificate is reproduced in Figure 7.2.

The Web conferencing system chosen for the course, called About, is relatively primitive. It only permits messages of less than 450 words, and does not support separation of the conference structure into Frames (as for example, the GEMBA system does). However, it does organise messages in threads and in addition to plain text, supports graphics and messages in HTML, thus allowing links to other sites.

The materials developed for the first two courses are almost exclusively text-based (there are one or two tables), and do not contain photos, graphics, video or audio. It is hoped that audio or videoconferencing might be used as a support medium at some point in the future. Due to the global spread of the programme, this will probably mean that Internet-based systems are the most feasible.

The multimedia course is more adventurous: the pedagogical approach here is the simulation of a company involved in the design and development of multimedia products using software available via the Web, collaboration between students through the running of 'production team meetings' via

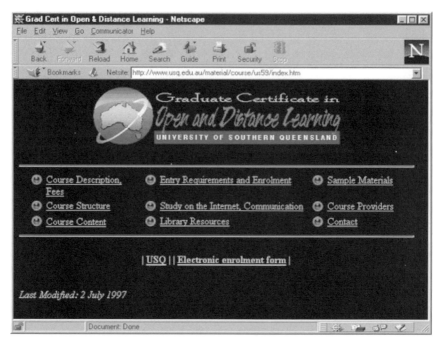

Figure 7.2 Homepage of USQ's Graduate Certificate

Internet Relay Chat, supplemented by RealAudio. The student projects prepared for this course in 1997 through collaboration amongst eighteen students in eleven countries, was considered superior to that of the same unit taught on campus (http://www.connect.usq.edu.au/students/d9710775/con 1.html). The 'entrance' to this multimedia course is reproduced in Figure 7.3.

Evaluation data

I became aware of the existence of this course in a way which exemplifies one of the central concerns of this book – the shifting paradigms in the establishment of quality standards in global, telecommunications-based education. I was invited to give a keynote address at a national conference for teachers and educationalists in Rio de Janeiro. Following my talk about new technologies for open and distance learning, a Brazilian girl came up to me and asked whether I had ever heard of the University of Southern Queensland. When I said that I had, she wanted to know my opinion of the institution and whether I thought it was a reputable organisation with a track record in the field of distance learning. Her employer was going to sponsor her to take the Certificate, but they laid down the condition that she resign from her supplementary job. In other words, she had to decide between extra income and further qualifications. What she was seeking from me was some basis for judging the value of the qualification in the wider world. As the global

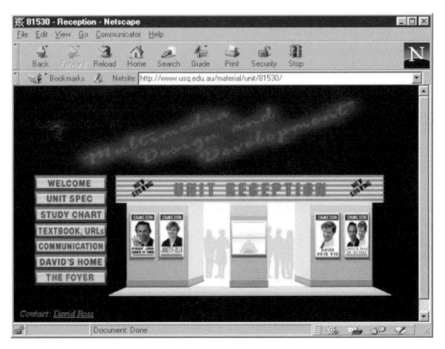

Figure 7.3 Web page from USQ's multimedia course

education phenomenon gathers momentum, this kind of search for quality guarantees will no doubt give rise to international providers of 'the good global courses guide'.

When I returned to my desk, I soon found an announcement of the Certificate on the Web, and contacted the author of the initial course, whom I already knew, to ask whether I could evaluate this global, web-based course for my book. All I knew about the programme was that 'the whole course' was to be web-based and that the student intake was intended to be global. I visited Toowoomba for three days just before the first two courses finished, and spoke to a wide range of the staff involved in producing the Certificate.

Student feedback

The first thing I discovered was that although twenty-two students had initially registered for the first course, only seven were active. The primary cause of the reduction was access problems. Indeed, my Brazilian friend never finally registered because of poor Internet connections. The three students in the Solomon Islands were experiencing considerable difficulties in logging on to the Web. The telephone system throughout the Islands is simply not good enough to support digital interaction (although there is a promise that this will improve in the next six months) and the high humidity there makes matters worse. The most active participants were those from Canada and the USA (as well as two from USQ). Several of the original twenty-two dropped out for the usual distance education reasons: unforeseen domestic or job problems, lack of time, and illness.

Another barrier for students proved to be access to the recommended readings. The Mexican students, for example, complained that they had great difficulty getting hold of them, and felt it should be part of the USQ's responsibility to provide them.

I inquired about cultural and second language issues and whether these had proved to be problems or advantages on the conference interactions. It would seem that the work produced by some of the second language users was very poor, and that writing and spelling were sloppy. There were genuine communications problems, partly linguistic and partly cultural, and undoubtedly the discussions were dominated by the English mother tongue participants. The tutor was concerned that correcting the language mistakes or pointing out errors would simply make matters worse.

There were no collaborative assignments or structured group activities in this first course; however, students were invited to comment on each other's reflections. Several participants were prolific in their use of conferencing and tended to dominate the discussions, clearly spending more than the ten–twelve hours a week suggested in the course requirements.

Naidu, the author and tutor of the course, has carried out a questionnaire evaluation of the students and staff involved in the project (Naidu, 1997). He reports the following responses from students, some of whom found adjusting to the demands of online interaction difficult:

> I found it very difficult to express my thoughts so publicly, not knowing anyone who was in the class and not knowing their backgrounds.
>
> (Naidu, 1997)

> The problem was more in my feeling that I needed to really reflect and read about the topic before I could say anything, and by the time I was ready to say something, people had moved on and it was too late, so I didn't contribute much to the discussions.
>
> (*ibid.*)

Nevertheless, there was general agreement that the use of the Web conferencing system for reflecting and conceptualising was valuable:

> Just sharing reflections with others was a valuable learning experience for me and one which has very important implications for the work that I am currently engaged in. Placing myself in the position of the student, experiencing all the fears and apprehensions arising from lack of knowledge and skill was a very, very important experience.
>
> (*ibid.*)

Finally, one student made a comment which really justifies the globalisation of courses such as this:

> Sometimes, somehow, a certain 'viewpoint or ethos' tends to become rooted in most teaching departments or faculty. The opportunity to be able to follow a course of study from a place far away from one's own workplace and the opportunity to interact with practitioners from other and especially distant places, and to be able to share their views and experiences is extremely valuable because it affords an appreciation of not only one's own but different and sometimes refreshing views and perspectives.
>
> (*ibid.*)

Faculty views

I asked the course tutor how much time he spent interacting with students throughout the duration of the course (a 120-hour course lasting ten weeks). He said that initially he would spend two–three hours per day responding to messages and refining the materials. Once the course attained a 'steady state', this reduced to one hour a day. By the end of the course, when students were completing their project, he logged on several times a week.

The other course, running concurrently, was less structured and more student-led, as a result of different faculty approaches to teaching and learning.

Students were expected to use the many resources provided from the Web pages. Fewer students were registered initially, however, and there was less use made of the conferencing system.

The library staff at USQ had clearly seen that the advent of Web-based courses was an opportunity for them to re-engineer their support mechanisms for the university. The faculty staff acknowledged that, 'the library has really gone ahead in leaps and bounds with this initiative'. As academics increasingly decide to use resource-based pedagogical approaches, library staff have a stronger role to play by developing expertise in online resources.

Institutional considerations

One of the institutional issues arising from this and other distance taught courses was that of 'rolling intake'. Should the institution move to a policy of allowing students to enrol at any time they want? Could they provide the infrastructure to support a rolling intake, and would the benefits of flexibility outweigh the loss of a coherent student body on any particular course? Set periods in which a course is offered obviously reduces its flexibility, and the more global the student market, the greater the appeal of a rolling intake. On the Certificate, for example, the first courses were offered during the summer vacation period in the Northern Hemisphere and this caused problems for the Canadian students particularly. However, the value of student interaction on a conferencing system is obviously reduced when other students are at different points in the course. Collaborative projects and activities are probably unworkable, as are structured discussions and guest lectures. Nevertheless, USQ was aware of growing pressure to respond to demands from the marketplace, and staff were keeping the issue under review.

Naidu's evaluation documents the interest of all members of the team involved in producing the Certificate: the IT staff who helped set up the conferencing and computer systems, the instructional design staff who welcomed the innovation, the library staff who were delighted to have an impact on the design and development of the courses from the beginning. I certainly found this to be the case in my discussions with them. It was clearly a positive experience for the staff involved.

Each faculty at USQ had prepared detailed plans for a general move to flexible delivery systems, involving multimedia CD-ROM, the Web, video and other computer-based systems. Many academics were keen to 'put their materials up on the Web'. A Masters degree in Professional Accounting went online in July 1997 and a whole faculty was providing online courses for 1998. The intention was to offer the traditional print-based courses as well as the web-based version, in order to attract the widest possible student base. However, there were other members of staff who were concerned about this approach. They realised that the Web is more than a delivery medium and teaching material designed for print does not translate to the Web successfully without undergoing a complete reconceptualisation. Online resources require regular updating; linear content must be rethought for hypertext, and online interaction needs a different support structure. The practice of developing and running the Certificate is an excellent learning experience for the institution as a whole, if the lessons can be disseminated throughout by evaluation and the infrastructure adapted to meet the new demands.

Analysis and conclusions

Benefits from global perspective

One of the problems with the first intake of students on the Certificate was that USQ had no control of the people nominated by the collaborating institutions to participate. There was some indication that a few participants had been told to take the Certificate or risk dismissal. Others volunteered out of curiosity. None were paying fees. In short, the student cohort began without ideal motivations for distance learning. This will probably change with the next intake of students who will be paying fees and will have chosen to take the Certificate for its intrinsic attractions.

Nevertheless, it would be hard to conclude that the majority of students on the first courses benefited from the global participation or that the course contents reflected a particularly global perspective. One student clearly did benefit, and points to the kind of outcome the courses could have for all the participants as Web access improves, institutional expertise develops, and the student body is more intrinsically motivated.

Technology strategy

The technology strategy of the Certificate represents the coal face of global delivery on the Web: access from the developing world is still unreliable. Sadly, as so often is the case, those who would most like to take global courses have least opportunity to do so.

Similarly, while the Web can deliver high quality multimedia and a stimulating environment for learning, global access restricts the use of its most engaging features, due to bandwidth considerations.

Pedagogical transformation

All of the courses on the Certificate are designed for the Web. Of the two courses I evaluated for this case study, I would call the first one a 'wrap-around model' (where the course material provides a framework around one or more set texts) and the other I would call a 'resource-based model' (where the course material provides a framework for the student to work with a range of electronic resources). These are appropriate uses of the medium and do extend the institution's range of pedagogical approaches to distance education into online delivery.

However, interaction through computer conferencing is a difficult medium to use tentatively – it is usually most successful educationally when it is central to a course, when online collaborative work is built into the teaching model, when structure is provided to the interactions, and when Web materials are integrated with the discussions. Students who are full-time staff at other institutions, and who are accessing the conferencing discussions on the margins of their working day, are a difficult constituency to turn into active online participants even with the best prepared conferencing activities. In this sense the strength of the Web and computer conferencing – convenience and flexibility – is also the primary weakness – neither demand the student's attention. Other more immediate events easily take precedence.

Institutional change

The Distance Education Centre is clearly leading the way in investigating new technology directions within USQ. Other faculties were aware of the need to update their uses of technology, but underestimated the effort and degree of change necessary to produce a high quality product with telecommunications media. The library was responding actively to the challenge of the new media and understood that the Web was not just a new delivery vehicle for distance education materials, but a whole new medium for designing courses.

My feeling is that this programme reflects many of the current problems with global courses:

- access to the Web is still problematic on anything resembling a global scale;
- many course providers have little experience in writing material for this new environment or in designing and running online interactive courses;
- students who enrol in professional updating courses have not developed the study patterns or the discipline to sustain participation in courses delivered with 'undemanding media';
- if cultural and linguistic differences are not addressed specifically by the course designers, Western English mother tongue students will inevitably dominate online discussions;
- institutions need to acquire expertise in the new media, and plunging in to small scale projects such as the Certificate is an obvious way to begin building up experience. The Web is full of such early offerings.

8 Jones Education Company
From TV to the Internet

Outline of the programme

The Mind Extension University, an early educational venture of Jones Education Company (JEC), has been re-launched under the name of Jones College Connection, as the company has moved on from the use of cable networks and TV broadcasting to the wider aim captured in their mission statement thus:

> To be the learning solution of choice for organizations, with global delivery of independent education and training content, and a focus on customized solutions and unparalleled support.

This approach arises from the allegiance of JEC to the notions of self-empowering knowledge and education available to adults at any time, and from anywhere.

The business is currently focused around five educational enterprises:

- JEC Knowledge TV: educational programming catering to the life-long learning market, targeting specific vocational and leisure areas, and acting as a promoter of their other four enterprises.
- JEC College Connection: the distance learning vehicle of JEC, connecting students to college courses, degree programmes and professional training from recognised universities, using videotape, the Internet, the Web, and television. In total, twelve universities offer more than 200 courses and a choice of ten degree programmes at associate, bachelor and master level. This includes a new International University programme offering an MBA and Bachelors in Business.
- JEC Knowledge Store: JEC's electronic retailer, offering more than 300 original videos, audios, books and CD-ROMs.
- JEC Knowledge Online: located at http://www.jec.edu/, this website provides information about the services of the company, as well as enrolments and network schedules for courses and programmes.
- Jones Computer Network: the first cable television network devoted to

computers and emerging technology. The programs are part entertainment, part information for adults ranging from the computer illiterate to the advanced user. Subjects include interactive multimedia reviews, computer purchasing tips and software demonstrations, as well as interviews with technology leaders.

The Company is inspired and directed by the vision of its chairman, Glenn Jones, who is an enthusiast both for technology and for the empowering potential of education. Figure 8.1 shows the JEC homepage.

Global reach

Over the last few years JEC has steadily marched across the globe creating partnerships and agreements to market their five educational enterprises in Asia, Europe, Latin America and soon, Africa, India and South America.

Knowledge TV's European roll-out began in the fall of 1996 with the launch of their computer and technology programming on Bell Cablemedia in Britain. The British launch was only the start of pan-European programming designed to meet a range of life-long learning needs.

Plans are in hand to extend this provision to cable Internet access, a broadband Internet service delivered over television cables to the home and offering much faster speeds than ISDN. 'Proponents of the technology believe it is the breakthrough that the Internet needs before it can become a mass medium like television' (Durham, 1996).

The argument is that if people are accessing the Internet from home at current slow speeds, many more will do so with the very fast speeds offered by

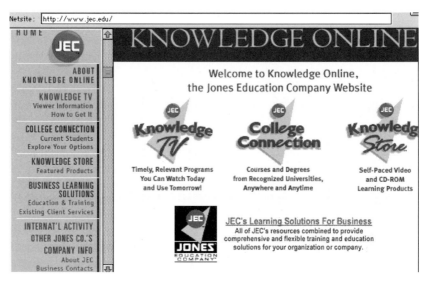

Figure 8.1 Jones Education Company homepage

cable. Jones himself believes that, 'speed is a product in itself and in the twenty-first century, the saving of time will identify good products' (*Financial Times*, 1996).

In January 1997, the same computer and technology programming went on air through China Education Television (CETV). This series is only the first phase in a broader understanding to provide computer, business and technical skills programming to China. The programming is produced in English and translated into Mandarin by CETV. The Asian market had previously adopted Knowledge TV programmes through cable and satellite companies in Hong Kong, South Korea, Thailand and Singapore.

The Company aims to cater for a wide range of adult education needs from practical information to formal degrees and certificates. While the Knowledge TV programmes are essentially stand-alone courses for self-study, JEC College Connection provides the formal arm of the equation through partnerships with educational providers. These programmes are not as extensive at the global level as the Knowledge TV applications, but a number of successful global programmes do exist and many more are in the pipeline. The company antici-pates that their non-US market will overtake their US market, and expanding further into international markets is one of their primary strategies.

In terms of this case study I intend to examine both the global Knowledge TV offerings of JEC and certain courses from the College Connection which have the most global components.

JEC Knowledge TV

Content

The foundation of the Knowledge TV programming is the designation of four target areas as the focus for all development. Based on market surveys, the four have been identified as:

- Business, careers, and finance – examples include professional and personal development programmes such as *The Art of Investing*, *Using the Internet in Business* and *Perfecting the Presentation*. The aim is for content that can immediately be applied on the job and in people's lives.
- Health and well-being – featuring health-related news, personal health care advice and consumer reports. Examples include *Alternative Medicine* and *Healthy Women 2000*.
- Global culture and language – reflecting the personal mission of Glenn Jones, this category concentrates on the teaching of language as the *sine qua non* of global communication.
- Computers and technology – covering the latest information on software, hardware, computer peripherals and technology news.

The Company claims that they are the only global provider of education which the viewer can 'watch today and use tomorrow to improve their quality of life'. How can they deliver this range of material in so many markets? The answer lies in their levels of customisation. 'The key to success in any market is being culturally and linguistically relevant. As we add countries, we will add levels of customization' (Amos, 1997).

I asked Amos about these levels of customisation. In certain countries (e.g. Poland and Romania), their research shows that dubbing is the right solution. In others (e.g. The Netherlands), subtitling is preferred. For Spanish-speaking countries they are working on complete translations of the programmes. As the market develops in particular countries, they will work with partners to commission local programmes.

I asked about the extent to which they saw themselves as marketing American culture and know-how. They have identified three areas of the content where the American approach is in demand: American culture, technology and business. In other areas, they intend to work with partners and local developers. Amos was certainly aware that English language broadcasting was only 'cream skimming', and that to really enter the market they would have to translate, version or commission locally.

Technology

Perhaps the most interesting of the findings to emerge from the JEC study was the company's attitude to delivery technologies for different countries. Whilst in the US market, the company was moving away from TV and video lectures on to the Internet and the Web; they perceived that the market in Asia and Latin America still favoured traditional TV lectures.

> In the US, the channel has moved away from offering courses on television, using complementary services such as the Internet and retail videos for most specific classes. But in Europe and Asia, customers are more interested in taking courses by TV.
>
> (Amos, 1997)

In Europe, the Knowledge TV was also seen as a vehicle for raising awareness of certified courses to be offered through College Connection. Furthermore, the notion of a video lecture was no longer an acceptable model for a TV programme, as video games, multimedia products and entertainment TV had set new standards for educational TV. This kind of programming is obviously more demanding and expensive to make.

JEC College Connection

Content

The certification side of the Jones offerings began through the Mind

Extension University programme which was operated primarily in the USA and primarily using the company's satellite network for delivery of course content. With the re-launch as JEC College Connection, the company re-positioned itself in order to distinguish its distance education programmes from its competitors by offering students the following elements:

- a variety of accredited universities and colleges from which to choose to earn a degree or certificate;
- a greater selection of degree and certificate programmes;
- greater flexibility in the scheduling and delivery methods for its courses;
- increased frequency in the delivery of its courses.

Having moved beyond the technology of video on cable television to embrace Internet technologies, the certification programme was easier to extend globally, or at least internationally. The flagship international programme is their Bachelor and Master of Arts in Business Communication offered by the International University College (IUC). IUC was founded by Glenn Jones in order to realise the changed economics of a virtual institution and to provide courses with specific learning outcomes. The curriculum was structured as a result of extensive consultation with trainers in major companies such as Ford Motor Company, AT&T, US West, and EDS (Witherspoon, 1997). One of the cornerstones of the programme is that students can begin a course at any time.

Technology

These programmes are delivered via video lectures which are extended, updated and supported by Web pages with details of assignments, references, case studies and links to the listserv discussions with the tutors and other students. A printed Study Guide is also available as an HTML document on the Web.

Around 200 students took these programmes during 1996, the majority on the Masters Degree. While the largest concentration of JEC students reside in Colorado and California, all fifty states have been represented as well as sixteen foreign countries. Proctored testing at a local location is the usual method of examination, although 'take home' testing is also used.

JEC provides the administrative support for courses – marketing, registering and handling fee payments and exam results. Many of these facilities are now accessible from their Web site (http://www.jec.edu/).

Evaluation data

My research on the JEC educational ventures has involved a range of telephone interviews, examination of extensive documentation provided by the company and reviewing Web sites and course evaluation questionnaires.

Student feedback

Flexibility is the main advantage of the IUC courses, as the students have a mean age between 26 and 45 with 65 per cent females. Typical feedback from students is the following:

> It is so accommodating. With all of my daughter's activities, trying to work my schedule around a traditional program would be impossible.

Interactive technologies, as we have seen so often elsewhere in these chapters, are changing the nature and status of distance education:

> The professors were very receptive and anxious to help. I never felt like I wasn't part of the class. I think I receive more help from my professors now than when I was taking courses on-campus.

Finally, as a means of providing life-long learning and professional updating, these programmes are already meeting the much hyped demands of the marketplace:

> I want to get into management with my current employer, but it's difficult to do without a degree. Now I have the chance to complete my degree at home and I hope to use it to advance in my career.

Interestingly, the most popular courses are those related to Business Uses of the Internet, Business Writing, and Team Effectiveness. Students clearly welcomed the high levels of online interaction and engagement, as well as the peer-to-peer learning activities based on small and large group discussions used on the IUC courses. The majority of students rated the courses as 'above their expectations'. On several courses, students were able to apply their learning immediately in the workplace, in ways that attracted the notice of their colleagues.

Evaluation questionnaires show that interaction with faculty ranged from daily to several exchanges per week. Most students gave their tutors ratings of either excellent or good. The Web pages accompanying the courses were also considered excellent.

Faculty views

The role of faculty on these courses is seen very much in the model of guide and facilitator, providing pacing for students at a distance and generating online interaction and participation in the group discussions. The Dean of Academic Programs of IUC writes in the Course Prospectus:

> We know from research that adults want convenience, flexibility and

information that is applicable to their daily personal and professional lives. IUC meets these needs by using a multiple media approach to the study of communication, which includes skills and knowledge that are critical for the 21st century.

The JEC staff whom I interviewed were keen to improve their systems for monitoring and evaluating the extent to which faculty were meeting such aims, and not to leave this to the university supplying the course. Plans were in hand to begin systematic evaluation studies.

I asked one of my interviewees a very direct question about the perceived view of educational providers like JEC 'undercutting' traditional universities by hiring academics to write courses for sums which did not cover the costs of academic research underwritten by universities. The response was that this kind of business practice would not work in the long term. The essence of the JEC approach was built on partnerships, which are only successful when both parties are happy with the arrangements. Unlike other providers, JEC does not sell their own degree, and are therefore reliant on the goodwill and good name of their partners. JEC noted a change over the last few years in attitudes by universities towards other educational providers. Even though the prestige universities would still prefer that the new providers did not exist, they were much more ready now than in the past to jump on the train rather than stand haughtily at the side as it hurtles by. Many were beginning to see collaborative ventures with the likes of JEC as an opportunity to bring in some marginal revenue.

With the Knowledge TV programmes, I asked about the issue of writing material suitable for a global audience. Again, as in other case studies, the response was that the 'one size fits all' approach was doomed to meeting no one's needs well, and to condemnation on all sides as bland and poor learning material. Versioning was the preferred solution by JEC with local providers complementing the programming.

Institutional considerations

Amos' view of broadcast TV as an educational medium for distance education courses was that it was inefficient and ultimately ineffective. Using a satellite or cable to deliver specialist courses to a targeted audience was inherently a poor use of the medium. For him, the Internet was a technological saviour: portable, user driven, flexible as to time and location, supportive of one-to-one, one-to-many and many-to-many learning models. He also found from feedback on courses that students want interaction with a tutor, to help them pace their studies and to keep engaged with the course. They did not need the teacher to deliver the content of the course, but rather to provide the support and guidance around it. The Internet offered many more opportunities for innovative course delivery than the TV lecture.

The corporate market was another target for JEC expansion. As the company moved on from being a 'one technology solution', the market for offering consultancy in designing training programmes was opening up – particularly for government, the military and industry. JEC saw their advantage as consultants in being able to offer independent content (using partners and special commissions) and advice on multiple delivery platforms (including global delivery through their own satellite systems), and extensive experience of creating and adapting specific content, tracking enrolments, credits and payments, and delivering course materials and supporting students by phone, Internet and fax.

Scott Kline, the Vice-President for Corporate Business Development, told me: 'Working with corporates will be a much bigger market for us ultimately than formal education. Consultancy – selling our expertise – is what will grow, not selling a technology'. He also noted that it was very difficult to make money in the CD-ROM market, unless the client was very large and needed standard products.

Analysis and conclusions

It would be easy to exaggerate the significance of the activities of JEC. It is still, by its own admission, a small player in both the educational scene and the global marketplace. By 1996 only 135 students had graduated from degree programmes, though 6,400 had completed courses over about eight years. Nevertheless, the directions, the attitudes and the development of JEC are clearly significant in the documentation of global education.

Benefits from global perspective

I think it would be fair to say that the main beneficiary of the global activities of JEC are JEC staff. In other words, the company is building up tremendous expertise in how to deliver education in many countries. Students may benefit indirectly from that expertise, but not directly from global content or interactions with students and tutors from around the world. Nevertheless, JEC is offering opportunities to educational partners in many countries to expand their offerings or delivery technologies. Knowledge TV is also providing educational opportunities of a kind and reaching people through mass media who would otherwise be unaware of or uninterested in formal academic programmes.

So far the international element of the JEC College Connection is hardly global in the sense in which I have been defining it throughout this book. In fact, the global component of courses offered through IUC is largely tokenism and consisting of the 'Americans living or moving abroad' sort, rather than genuine non-nationals. Still, it is early days for the JEC College Connection, and its plans for developing programmes in other countries are ambitious.

Technology strategy

I think the migration from satellite and cable TV to multiple delivery plat-forms is very significant. The idea of broadcast TV as a mass medium for raising awareness and for marketing a more formal product delivered through other media is a lesson the UKOU learned many years ago. The fact that their investigations have led them to continue the use of video lectures in Asia is also notable. I have ascribed this, in earlier chapters, to the pedagog-ical tradition of teacher-centred learning. It may, however, have more to do with the greater availability of home computers in the US that the company has moved to other technologies. Countries such as Singapore, which is also technology-rich, will be interesting to watch in drawing conclusions about whether the acceptability of TV lectures arises primarily from technology or from pedagogy.

The notion of designing a training programme around users' needs rather than around one particular technology is the cornerstone of any advice on best practice in the educational use of technology. Their belief in the market for consultancy rather than technology solutions is also a lesson other pioneers in the field would endorse.

Pedagogical transformation

I was interested in the content areas JEC identified as most marketable. They largely confirmed my own findings about the kinds of courses most commonly offered electronically and globally (business studies at all levels, computer related courses, and languages).

It is no secret that the traditional universities frequently disparage the quality of education offered by the new providers, such as JEC. The irony is, of course, that these providers are generally using the same staff and course designers, whose full-time employment is with traditional universities. While there is more to education than course content, and universities feel they provide a rich educational environment, informed by research, supported by library resources, and enlivened by the campus togetherness, it is clear that many students are benefiting equally from the convenience, relevance and interaction provided by companies such as JEC. Another irony centres on the theoretical versus practical divide. All of the JEC literature emphasises the relevance of their offerings to the workplace and to people's daily lives. Universities often take a 'holier than thou' attitude to such an objective, advo-cating that only with strong theoretical underpinnings can students be considered graduates of a subject. Obviously there is room in the market for both kinds of courses, but it would be even better if course providers learned from each other how to produce courses which stimulated and engaged students while providing a rounded exposure to the subject.

JEC is fully aware of the importance of choosing good partners to provide the content of their courses. Their choice is limited, however, by the attitude of conventional course providers and the extent to which the best institutions are prepared to collaborate. It will be interesting to see whether the partners who come forward to work with JEC in other countries are any different from those in the USA.

Institutional change

Over the last few years JEC has re-positioned itself in three significant ways:

- It has moved from targeting primarily the individual consumer of knowledge products to the corporate customer wanting tailored training solutions.
- It has begun to consolidate as a serious business, based on the vision of its founder, but developing into a player operating on the global stage.
- It has grown out of its cable network roots into other technologies and a broader view of educational provision.

9 IBM global training and education

Background

IBM is the world's largest training provider. Its materials consist primarily of subjects related to the computer and computing, but the 'softer subjects' such as management, sales, process and risk management, account for at least one third of the total coverage. Most of this training (about 80 per cent) is carried out face-to-face in locations around the world, and the rest consists largely of self-study materials in the form of multimedia CD-ROMs. IBM operates one of the world's largest data networks – the IBM Global Network. It provides truly global capabilities and is accessible from hundreds of cities worldwide. It provides a full range of network services including leased line and dial access, multiprotocol solutions and wireless communications.

This case study describes both the training IBM carries out for its own staff around the world, and the ways in which IBM supports education and training by other providers.

IBM used to operate on a devolved model in each country in which it had a presence. This led to a lot of inefficiencies as developments in one country (software, training solutions, course materials) were duplicated in another with little consistency. Recently this model has been replaced by a global curriculum model in which training materials are developed on an industry rather than country basis. Core components are designed across the whole sector with appendices for each country to address specific differences (e.g. in banking arrangements).

Related to this change is the announcement last year of the IBM Global Campus, as the user interface to distance learning solutions for the higher education sector and for business professionals. The Global Campus is not based on a particular technology; rather, it is an architecture providing an end-to-end solution for education and training needs. For example, it includes tools for administration and management, for course development, for learner support, exploration and guidance. More importantly, it allows users to integrate their own facilities and software. It is still under development, and was being used with internal staff during 1997, and will have external clients thereafter. Figure 9.1 shows the concept graphically.

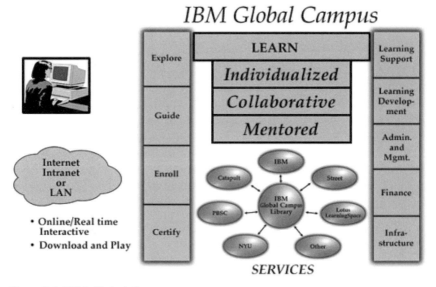

Figure 9.1 IBM Global Campus

ThinkPad University is another IBM initiative. This involves much more than giving notebook computers to everyone on campus. Planning is part of the package: reviewing existing campus facilities and project management, developing a campus infrastructure that supports mobile computing, as well as training faculty in how to use technology in their teaching. The first fully electronic campus in Canada is Acadia University in Nova Scotia, which chose the ThinkPad University approach to integrate computers into the whole teaching and learning environment, and to equip every student, by the year 2000, with an IBM ThinkPad notebook computer.

Importance of training

After the company had been through a period of severe downsizing recently (from 400,000 to 200,000), a big training initiative was instituted for the staff who remained in order to fill in the skills gap. A new approach to training was part of the initiative. Under the old model, the line manager was responsible for the training programme for each member of staff in the department. In the new model, each person takes far greater responsibility for the development of their skills and for transferring those skills into the workplace. More emphasis is placed on self-study carried out in the employee's own time. The Global Campus includes features to support this: skills assessment, goal analysis and personalised road maps to help learners make the most effective use of their training time.

During the first phase of the use of Global Campus, one internal division of IBM is acting as the pilot for the rest of the company. By the end of 1997, all IBM staff were using the system to 'mediate' their training needs.

The use of technology

IBM used to operate a satellite system for training its own employees. In 1993 it was shut down due to lack of use. Staff were either not showing up for their training sessions or were falling asleep in the room. There is still some use made of the system for their employees in Asian countries, but on the whole the company's reaction is that training needs to be more interactive and more learner-centred. IBM's recent acquisition of Lotus Development Corporation provides, through Lotus Notes software, the technology for the move towards this interactive approach. IBM trainers have learned the importance of making the technology easily accessible to the end user – preferably on their desk. They are also convinced of the value of team work as part of the learning environment.

In three to four years, IBM expects to have moved from 80 per cent face-to-face training to 20 per cent face-to-face with the remainder in various forms of stand-alone and distributed distance learning. The company also see mixed modes of delivery, which may contain a face-to-face component, becoming the standard.

As the bandwidth increases, IBM expects to make much greater use of video on the network (Internet or Intranet). In the meantime, it is experimenting with Web-casting as a way of providing real time video interaction.

Translating training materials

IBM has learned lessons about translation of its training materials. First of all, for internal training, as English is the company language, it wants its employees to be able to operate in English. The solution often used is to provide an instructor speaking in the local language, but the handout material is in English. For external training courses, IBM considers itself exceptional in the amount of training materials it supplies in languages other than English (although this applies almost exclusively to computer-related subjects, not to the 'soft subjects'). In order to carry out multiple translations (at least twelve languages), the company has developed a template approach for preparing multimedia training materials. Most of this translation is carried out by Polar Bear Systems Corporation, now owned by IBM. Because the content has a high level of consistency and a relatively narrow scope, it is efficient for the system to store materials in small chunks, which can be re-used across and within programmes. This reduces the translation requirements. Nevertheless, as the amount of video and audio in the multimedia increases, much of this will have to be outsourced, the Polar Bear spokesperson told me.

LearningSpace

The Global Campus uses Lotus LearningSpace, a Notes R4 application, to deliver networked, instructor-led, collaborative learning. It accomplishes this through specialised interactive modules which enable the learner to interact with course materials, each other and the instructor in a distributed learning environment. This asynchronous delivery platform enables team-based activities and discussion with the full power of Notes and its functionality. Through the application of Domino server technology, it is possible to host LearningSpace directly on the Web. In addition, other IBM developments and alliances will provide enhanced multimedia content delivery through streaming and other compression technologies.

IBM representatives explained their approach as follows:

> We believe that a fully-integrated learning solution must address major functions including: explore, guide, enrol, finance, learn, certify, learning support, learning development, administration and management, and infrastructure. Based on our analysis of learners and the learning experi-ence across many environments, these functions reflect the core learning services and activities provided by course developers, instructors, training organizations, and administrators. IBM plans to address each of these strategic functions through IBM Global Campus and its supporting services and products.
>
> (http://www.ibm.com)

Exemplars

I have chosen two initiatives to investigate for this case study. One is an example of an IBM client using Lotus LearningSpace to underpin a new initiative on the global learning stage. This is Magellan University. My second example is a training programme for IBM staff run by the Business School of the Open University.

Magellan University

Magellan University is a privately funded, for-profit corporation, set up with the guiding principle, 'Excellence in education, anywhere, any time'. While primarily US-based at the moment, it clearly has global aspirations.

The distinguishing feature of the Magellan environment is the division of course content (consisting of video recordings of outstanding teachers) and course support (consisting of classes of about fifteen students managed by a tutor using Lotus Notes/Domino software).

As a new institution, Magellan is free to find its faculty from around the world, selecting them on the basis of their teaching excellence. The tutors are paid on a per student basis, and are expected to interact asynchronously with students, as well as to mark their assignments. Courses are offered in five- or eight-week formats throughout the year and consist of about sixty half-hour lectures and fifteen hours of online interaction.

The Electric Library consists of over 400 online lessons developed initially by the Plato Laboratory at the University of Illinois. Each lesson takes between one and two hours, and includes examples and self-tests. They are aimed at life-long learners wanting to brush up their knowledge of particular subject areas, or get a taste of new subjects. These online lessons are available to those who register and pay a monthly subscription, or alternatively are free to those who register for a particular course.

Other attributes of the traditional campus are replicated electronically: the online student union provides clubs, chat rooms, and discussion forums; advising, admissions, and registration are available twenty-four hours a day, and after registering for a course, the student receives print and video materials within forty-eight hours.

Magellan planning documents outline the pedagogical framework underpinning the approach (quoted from Witherspoon, 1997, p. 161, and see http://magellan.edu):

- Students will use the communication and collaborative work tools of the computer and the network in all classes. This, along with an abundance of work related problem solving as part of the regular class, will provide students with real-life skills necessary for the information age.
- Writing is an integral part of all courses. The ability to produce clear, well-written material is vital to success in any field of endeavour.
- Presentations to the class are expected in most courses. The ability to communicate effectively and persuade groups of people is vital to success in any field of endeavour. Presentations occur quite effectively via the Internet.

Unfortunately for this case study, it is somewhat premature to obtain evaluation data from Magellan courses. Nevertheless, I think it is possible to highlight a number of issues which are highly relevant to this study of global education more generally.

First of all, the course delivery strategy, while very simple, is not one-dimensional. That is, LearningSpace supports the online interaction and the administrative facilities and provides the interface to other resources, but the vital component of the course content is delivered by videocassette and CD-ROM. Magellan is also seeking to develop a learning channel (direct-to-home satellite broadcasting) in partnership with traditional academic institutions. In addition to carrying the video lectures, the channel will also carry a range of educational materials, performances, debates, etc.

Second, in the details I have provided about this new initiative, it is obvious that it addresses issues central to the growth of global education: client-centred short courses, available in a just-in-time format, with high quality content and small group support and, finally, flexibility of access.

Third, the cost structure of this institution is obviously very different from a traditional university.

It is projected Magellan's costs will be about 20 percent of those required for a conventional campus. Indeed, a Magellan analysis shows a total budget of $105 million to serve 30,000 FTE students, vs $700 million for a traditional campus.

(Witherspoon, 1997, p. 162)

However, apart from dispensing with buildings, Magellan also has dispensed with research. The best teachers, whose research, reputations and experience have been developed at traditional institutions, are bought in by Magellan at a fraction of the cost it takes to nurture that expertise. Already there are instances of faculty members advertising their availability to teach such courses (Hiltz, 1997). Whatever this points to about the future of research and its integration with teaching, we must acknowledge the power of market forces. Magellan is aimed at meeting a particular educational demand, and most certainly not at maintaining the status quo of traditional universities.

IBM management courses

In 1996 IBM (Europe) made an agreement with the Open Business School (OBS) for the training of a very large number of its managers. The first cohort consisted of 280 students including fifty in South Africa, some in Russia, and others in the Middle East, and the number continues to rise with each subsequent cohort. Students study the standard print-based course material, but additional day schools are held specifically for IBM managers. Apart from these, IBM students mix with other OBS students online and at tutorials.

The technology used on these additional day schools is the subject of this analysis. Developed by the Knowledge Media Institute (KMi) at the Open University, the KMi Stadium is designed to provide lectures, tutorials and workshops to dispersed but networked participants. Stadium events involve live audio illustrated with slides or other material, and feedback from participants via Web forms. Two events have been held so far: the first was a talk on finance given by an academic from OBS, and the second was a 'pub quiz' run as an exam revision session (see Figure 9.2).

For the first event, IBM managers were gathered in several locations for the Web-casting, whereas for the pub quiz, IBMers logged on individually or in very small groups. Working in teams, they answered the questions posed by the lecturer back at the Open University. Each team could see the scores, which were graded and posted during the event. Figure 9.3 shows details of the event as it appeared to the participants.

In both cases, however, technical failures dogged the events and detracted from their overall success. Feedback from the evaluation of the events shows that participants valued the content of the lecture and enjoyed the interactivity of the pub quiz. Interestingly, there was a noticeable difference in reaction to the technology between the Moscow managers and the, admittedly much smaller, non-Moscow-based participants. The Moscow students were

Figure 9.2 KMi Pub Quiz

Source: KMi Stadium and the developments from it, such as Pub Quiz, are the work of the following Open University staff: Peter Scott, Tony Seminara, Mike Wright, Mike Lewis, Andy Rix and Marc Eisenstadt.

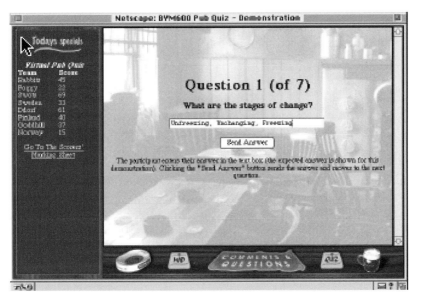

Figure 9.3 KMi Pub Quiz details

Source: KMi Stadium and the developments from it, such as Pub Quiz, are the work of the following Open University staff: Peter Scott, Tony Seminara, Mike Wright, Mike Lewis, Andy Rix and Marc Eisenstadt.

not impressed with the Stadium lecture, and said they did not enjoy taking part. The other students were much more positively disposed towards the technology and what it had to offer for their studies (Mulholland and Tyler, 1997).

What can we learn from this application of experimental Web-casting? First of all, the technology to support it is still immature, and second, not all learners are prepared to overlook difficulties in estimating the value of an educational event. My own estimation is that this technology has tremendous potential, especially for supporting global teaching. The fact that the material can be accessed after the event, and that it can support a range of teaching modes, from the large scale lecture to the intimate seminar, makes it a versatile medium for course delivery.

Conclusions

It seems obvious that a company such as IBM should use the technologies it is developing to sell to others, to train its own employees. Nevertheless, I have observed on several occasions, companies which market videoconferencing systems or telecommunications or computers, persisting in face-to-face training for their own staff. IBM is developing the Global Campus first in-house.

Despite the attempt in Global Campus to develop a cradle-to-grave system which supports all aspects of the education process, it is interesting that education providers are resistant to putting the whole of their technology delivery strategy into one basket. The Magellan University exemplifies that in this case study, but there are many other examples of technology diversity throughout the book. Whether this diversity is driven by pedagogical concerns, or by fear of being dependent on one technology provider, is not always clear.

IBM is an obvious collaborator for global education providers. It offers technology, software, networking capability, training materials and global know-how.

10 The UK Open University

From national to global education provider

Outline of the globalising process

Throughout the 1990s, the UKOU has been systematically changing itself into a global institution. It has probably invested more than any other established university, certainly in the UK, to re-engineer itself for the challenges of the new education market, and has transformed itself into a global education provider using a range of technologies and methods of operating in different countries. Nevertheless, its origins as a print-based, mass distance education system using supported open learning continue to dominate its approach.

Early developments

Tait (1996) notes the ways in which the UKOU was surreptitiously catering for students abroad almost from its inception: students could live abroad as long as they had a UK address for posting materials, and various schemes existed to register nationals abroad in the armed services or in Brussels. The latter schemes involved the recruitment of local representatives for managing, counselling and tutoring, but students continued to pay in sterling and 'were not completely accepted as a legitimate part of the University, but rather were tolerated as participants in a special scheme' (Tait, 1996, p. 55). Tait goes on to document two factors which marked a change in the attitude of the University towards internationalisation:

- the Open Business School (OBS), having become the largest business school in the UK, perceived that a potentially significant market existed in Europe;
- the OU's Student Association became increasingly well organised and student representatives outside the UK began complaining about their second class treatment.

With the endorsement and active support of senior management, the OU developed a network of physical centres throughout Europe, and in the case of the OBS, in Eastern Europe as well. Collaboration with other European distance teaching universities was sought in order to share study centre accommodation. Specialised staff development was offered to the tutors and counsellors hired locally, and OU academic staff made visits to all centres. Problems included the need to understand and comply with local employment regulations and salaries, which were sometimes higher than OU standards in the UK.

> As the OU expanded into other countries, instructors began to be paid in the local currency. This innovation created new challenges for the Finance Division, which had to initiate systems that would allow transactions in the whole range of European currencies, including ecus. However, the change reflected the move from a domestic style of operation to an international one. The same change was permitted for students: for the first time, they were allowed to pay their fees in the local currency.
>
> (Tait, 1996, p. 59)

As most continental students could not receive the OU's TV and radio broadcasts, it was decided that video and audio cassettes would be sent, along with the printed course materials. However, customs officers in a number of countries would not release the cassettes to students – at least not without additional taxes. This was despite the supposed free movement of goods and services within the European Union.

Initially the internationalisation of the OU was seen as providing education for the expatriate community living abroad (and to a lesser extent other Anglophones). This policy did not challenge the British orientation of the course materials. However, as experience of marketing the courses in other countries increased, and as the students who registered for courses broadened from Anglophones to Anglophiles, young people and the business and scientific community, it became apparent that this policy was no longer appropriate. Nevertheless, though the student population has broadened, the internationalisation of the curriculum has lagged behind. On most courses, it consists of the following:

* the use of case studies from outside the UK;
* an awareness of the need to restrict jargon and avoid UK references and examples;
* particular scrutiny of assignment and examination questions for ambiguity and national context.

The 1990s also saw the growth of asynchronous computer conferencing as one of the most common technologies for supporting OU students in the UK. The OU went to great lengths to provide local call access to students throughout the country, as feedback continued to show that differential call charges were a barrier to use. Making the same arrangements throughout Europe called for even greater efforts, as European Internet providers were non-existent or non-reliable. In early trials, the University simply paid for students' long distance charges, in order to provide the 'same service' abroad.

Developing a global strategy

The 're-engineering' process began in January 1994 with the announcement of the Vice-Chancellor's INSTILL programme, which amongst other strategies enabled the hiring of nearly forty academic staff with dual expertise in subjects across the curriculum and in the teaching of that subject through new technologies. Other elements of the programme included training for existing staff, the establishment of a new technology research centre called the Knowledge Media Institute, and a number of initiatives for global expansion. This was followed shortly by a programme to re-design the computer systems underpinning the management of all administrative support of the 150,000 students, in order to extend electronic interactions with students from the educational to the administrative level. It also allowed for the complexities which a global student body would bring; for example, adding flexibility to the fields which coded student data to cope with non-UK telephone numbers and addresses.

At senior level, the responsibilities of the five pro-vice chancellors of the University were reorganised to establish one which was dedicated to the development of a technology strategy for the preparation and delivery of courses. Through this office, many new projects have been funded to research, evaluate and develop appropriate technologies, software, and electronic support systems. Examples include: adaptations of RealAudio software to support tutorials and global lectures, developments to integrate Web, CD-ROM and computer conferencing systems, evaluation of technology delivered resource-based learning approaches, systems to support electronic submission and marking of student assignments, and structures to make institutional research materials available electronically throughout the organisation. All of these are in tune with the changes in both the domestic market (where evaluation shows that students want more flexibility in support systems) and the global market (where technology is essential to the delivery and administration of courses).

In 1996, the Open University Worldwide (OUW) was established to:

> meet the supported open learning needs of students and educational or training organisations worldwide by helping the Open University to become the leading quality provider of learning opportunities, distance teaching methodologies, materials and intellectual property.

One of the purposes for seeking new markets abroad was to reduce the University's reliance on government funding, which is set for steady decline throughout the foreseeable future. However, other benefits are seen as equally important:

- it will encourage acceleration of the development of new ways to service students' needs;
- it will contribute to the re-engineering process by focusing attention on methods of course development and quality assurance;
- it will offer opportunities for synergy with academics from other cultures and for two-way transfer of academic and pedagogic expertise;
- it will facilitate the extension of the curriculum into new areas and the adaptation of courses to meet new needs.

Existing global activities

The OU has adopted very different methods of operating in different countries. I will highlight some of the most significant:

- In Singapore about 6,000 students are studying with the Open University, in conjunction with its partner, Singapore Institute of Management, which carries out the marketing, local pricing and fee collection, registration, record keeping, employment of tutors, organisation of local support services and tutorial meetings. The UKOU retains responsibility for the content of courses, for tutor training, development and monitoring, for assessment and examination standards generally and for determining awards and appeals.
- A variant on the Singapore model operates in the countries of Central and Eastern Europe, where similar contractual relationships are in place – albeit mainly with commercial partners – but where the courses are offered in the local language. Special arrangements are therefore in place for monitoring academic quality (i.e. translation of some scripts so that UKOU staff can read them).
- In Hong Kong, the OU operates through the Open University of Hong Kong, which has about 20,000 students on courses for their own degrees and awards, the majority of them on courses which were acquired from the UKOU. In this model the local institution makes the adaptations of the assessment questions, tutor training material or course content to suit their own needs.
- A number of aid-funded projects are underway as part of the University's commitment to enabling access to higher education by those with very limited means. So, for example, the MBA programme has been delivered to 115 heads of state in Ethiopia and to a similar number of ministers and senior government officers in Eritrea.
- The undergraduate programme has been available to students across Continental Western Europe (CWE) and Ireland for some years. In 1996, over 6,000 students were registered, studying primarily in the Arts, Business School, Social Science and Mathematics. The majority lived in Ireland, Belgium, Germany, The Netherlands, Switzerland and France. All of the students in this programme study the same course at the same

time as their UK counterparts – where numbers allow, local tutors are hired and local tutorials are held. Otherwise students join UK-based tutor groups. Some of the courses have a compulsory online component in which CWE students interact with students in the UK.

- Starting in 1997, the MBA and subsequently other courses are being delivered through collaborative schemes in India and the USA.
- Joint course development will feature in the collaboration with the University of Waterloo in Canada, and in addition, the use of OU TV programmes broadcast on nation-wide cable TV will extend the OU's opportunities in Canada.

Few other organisations have the range of high quality teaching materials in print, audio and video which the OU has developed over many years, and which are now at the heart of its global enterprises. In addition, its know-how in delivering and administering courses on a vast scale is expertise in high demand.

With such a range of global practice, it has been difficult to select a few applications for evaluation and analysis. In the end, I have chosen three examples to illustrate three strategic aspects of global education:

- adaptations of a programme to meet different demands in different countries, which is best exemplified in the activities of the Open Business School;
- development of technology systems to support large scale courses electronically, which is best exemplified in a suite of computer courses, called MZX;
- a programme developed specifically for a global market and delivered largely online, which is best exemplified by the Institute of Educational Technology's new Masters of Open and Distance Education.

Open Business School

Content

The OBS has led the OU in its global developments, largely because the competition in the UK for business courses is much fiercer than in any other curriculum area. Currently there are 109 competitors offering part-time MBAs in the UK, whereas in science subjects, say, the UKOU easily has 75 per cent of the market in part-time undergraduate degrees.

The primary strategy of OBS is to use the global market to leverage economies of scale. While the Business School goes to some lengths to version and adapt its material for each new country, on the whole a small number of very successful courses forms the core of its business. The OBS boasts the highest completion rates of any part-time or distance taught MBA. The content does not try to be 'international'; rather, country-specific examples and case studies are used in order to clarify and make relevant to the student abroad the processes of British management thinking which is the selling point of the degree. A student/tutor ratio of sixteen to one, and the facilities for contacting tutors directly are other aspects of the approach which account for its success as the largest business school in the UK, and as the leader in the globalisation of the OU. As one of the senior academics explains it:

> This expansion has created enormous pressure within the School and the University, both in terms of understanding the needs of different customers and users, and in reconciling these needs with the systems and processes of the University. The success of the international expansion is a result of hard work and innovative thinking on the part of many people within the School. By appointing individual academics, course managers and administrators to take responsibility for each project we have succeeded in establishing clear accountability which has enabled us, generally speaking to implement international projects on time and in accordance with our commitments.
>
> (Stapleton, 1997)

The School is open to the possibility of allowing Europeans to write examinations in their native language, as feedback shows that taking these in English is a much bigger barrier than studying or writing assignments in English. So far, the OUBS Certificate and Diploma courses have been translated into six languages.

While the majority of OBS students are individuals studying from home, the School is increasingly expanding its work with the corporate sector. The arrangements with IBM, referred to in Chapter 9, are one example.

Technology

In addition to print, video and audio cassettes, the OBS makes substantial use of computer conferencing, both for teaching and for supporting students at a distance. Collaborative activities across business sectors are used on some courses, online tutorials and electronic guest lecturers are used on others. A particularly effective online training programme for both students and tutors has been devised in order to assist everyone to become an active user (Salmon and Giles, 1997). Recently considerable effort has been applied to supporting an online alumni programme to maintain the network of contacts developed as students. Many graduates of the MBA go on to become enthusiastic tutors for the School.

The Web is also being developed as a marketing and information tool for OBS courses, though its use across the whole spectrum of courses is still limited. Web-casting both in lecture mode and for small group tutorials is also being trialled, along with other synchronous whiteboarding software. As in the OU undergraduate programme, CD-ROM is used where it fulfils particular needs for providing large amounts of reference material, simulations and video and audio materials. The large numbers of students studying the courses over several years justifies the investment needed for developing high quality multimedia materials.

MZX courses

Content

The Computing Department has been developing a learning environment for the last two years to support the whole instruction process from teaching to administration through electronic communication. These systems have been piloted on an entry level and an upper level computing course, involving 350 students and twenty-three experienced tutors in 1996, and rising to nearly double that in 1997. Some of the students in these trials have been resident in the USA, Malaysia and New Zealand as well as continental Europe.

The aim of the development process has been to transform, not merely to translate, the current paper and face-to-face tutorial system to the electronic medium. The course team says:

> Many institutions are converting lecture notes or other paper based materials to HTML for the Web, but with little support provided for the student, the gains are minimal. Simply translating material from familiar media into electronic form is rarely productive – and is certainly inadequate for supported distance education, which aims to engage the student in a 'community of learning'. If we hope to improve rather than translate, we must understand the whole teaching and support process through a critical examination of its functions.
>
> (Petre *et al.*, 1997)

The key to transforming the presentation of the course is to add value for the student to compensate for the inevitable disadvantages of using technology. One of the ways in which electronic tutoring can add value to the students' experience of face-to-face problem solving sessions is to use the storage and access facilities of online systems to share tutors' support materials and dialogues with students amongst the whole student body as archives of these build up. Tutors also can use this breadth of material to address individual needs and thus exploit the expertise of their colleagues to reduce their own workload.

Technology

The key technology elements in the development process were:

• Systems to support interaction among students and tutors which can cater for students regardless of their location and the speed of their network connection or software available; thus the Web-based discussion system had a facility for receiving each item as email for those without good Web access.

• Assignment marking by tutors on screen with an electronic marking tool which allows the tutor to delete or insert text in any font or format (the inserted text appears in blue and the deleted text is displayed with a red strike-through), to add check marks and crosses and to provide annotations in a kind of hypertext comment appearing in a separate frame. Marks for each question are entered by the tutor but added by the system to produce the final grade.

• Electronic submission by the student and handling by administrators of assignments, which reduces the return time to students, particularly those living abroad, and also reduces (if not eliminates) minor administrative errors currently affecting half a million assignments.

• Synchronous and asynchronous Internet-based problem sessions which substitute for face-to-face tutorials, using email and Internet Relay Chat discussions.

Another more experimental area of development within the MZX trials is electronic examinations – specifically with global take-up in mind. In the first trial abroad, still using a proctored model, a copy of the exam paper was sent electronically to the sites abroad. The student at each site answered the questions directly on computer and returned the paper electronically. A proctor was present during the whole period and the subject of the examination was computing, so this was not a model which scales up easily to large numbers or perhaps to all areas of the curriculum. Nevertheless, it represents a start on one of the intractable problems of global delivery.

Masters in Open and Distance Education

Content

Some of the modules of this Masters Degree were developed in conjunction with Deakin and the University of South Australia under the arrangement that the UKOU would not accept students from Australia in exchange for joint use of the materials. Another agreement is being developed in conjunction with Florida State University. The UKOU course is tutored entirely online using a Web-based conferencing system and requires students to submit their work throughout the programme into a conference accessible for comment by their tutor and other students. The second year of the course concerns applications of electronic media in distance education and is carried out largely online. Collaborative projects such as making a Web site, taking part in a debate, analysing and commenting on multimedia materials, Web resources and online articles, form the content of the course. In one assignment, students are marked on their ability to refine a previous assignment in the light of comments from their tutor and other students. Each person is required to comment on several other assignments as part of their work.

While numbers on the courses remain between fifty and 100, the tutoring will be carried out by central members of staff in the department. Current enrolment is roughly half UK-based and the other half from all parts of the world (except Australia).

Much of the expertise in designing and tutoring online courses has been built up in the department through many years of running 'train-the-trainer' courses on a global scale in the use of new educational media using the FirstClass computer conferencing system and latterly a Web-based system. This has given staff the opportunity to refine techniques for engaging students in successful online interactions, for designing structures and collaborative exercises which work online and for handling cultural problems sensitively.

Technology

The Masters Degree is using the electronic assignment marking and submission system designed by the MZX course team outlined above. With students so dispersed around the globe (but few in each country) providing local support and using print and postal systems would have been terribly costly and unwieldy.

In addition to access to the Internet, students need a CD-ROM drive to use a database of research articles in the first year, and a series of multimedia clips in the second. Web pages carry much of the content of the second year modules and browsing external sites forms a critical component of the activities.

The Web conferencing system used for discussions has been adapted in a number of ways to provide features demanded by the course team for supporting truly online course delivery. For example, the threading system for messages was improved to make the commenting structure more obvious, and a feature was added to allow the user to see who has read a particular message. Figure 10.1 shows the system as developed for the 1997 presentation.

Evaluation data

As a member of staff of the UKOU and, furthermore, situated in the department which carries out evaluation for the University, I have obviously had easy access to a very wide range of data for presenting this case study. Nevertheless, I interviewed a number of senior staff, primarily regarding their views of the University's globalising processes. I have also interviewed students both by telephone and by email on many occasions across many courses to ascertain their views of the University's use of new technology.

Student feedback

The students on the three programmes I have described above represent

○ #465 <u>**GREAT STUFF!**</u> 23/5/97, David
  ○ #480 <u>**silent majority**</u> 24/5/97, Helenc
    ○ #519 <u>**Who else is out there--**</u> 28/5/97, Alistair
    ○ #538 <u>**Course statistics**</u> 30/5/97, David
      ○ #556 <u>**Thank you**</u> 31/5/97, Helenc
      ○ #557 <u>**Sometimes late TMAs - problems with Webforms**</u> 1/6/97, Johnn
        ○ #576 <u>**40 minutes of your life gone**</u> 3/6/97, David
      ○ #560 <u>**Photos and biographies**</u> 2/6/97, Belindap
        ○ #561 <u>**Snapshots**</u> 2/6/97, Jenniferg
        ○ #570 <u>**to see or not to see**</u> 3/6/97, Helenc
          ○ #575 <u>**seeing is believing?**</u> 3/6/97, Simonr
            ○ #581 <u>**almost the same issue ...**</u> 3/6/97, Simonr
            ○ #582 <u>**almost the same issue ...**</u> 3/6/97, Simonr
            ○ #587 <u>**books without ears**</u> 3/6/97, Helenc
            ○ #588 <u>**books without ears**</u> 3/6/97, Helenc
            ○ #589 <u>**books without ears**</u> 3/6/97, Helenc
            ○ #590 <u>**BBB's without brains!**</u> 3/6/97, Helenc
            ○ #594 <u>**almost the same issue ... (third try lucky?)**</u> 4/6/97, Simonr
              ○ #598 <u>**Flaming cheek! An Intellectual Approach**</u> 4/6/97, Johnn
      ○ #577 <u>**Photos and pen sketches**</u> 3/6/97, David
        ○ #578 <u>**Posterity Messages**</u> 3/6/97, Stuartn
        ○ #579 <u>**Posterity Messages**</u> 3/6/97, Stuartn

Figure 10.1 IET MA threaded messages

distinct categories: undergraduates in the case of the computer courses, busy executives in the case of OBS students, and professionals at universities and training organisations around the world in the case of the MA. These categories have implications for the use of new technologies:

- whether students are logging on from home, where access is relatively poor and the student is paying the phone charges, or from work, where access is usually relatively good and moreover is free to the student;
- the level of self-confidence and the sophistication of the student's self-directed learning approach affects their use of online systems – some remain passive lurkers, others become active and interactive participants;
- the greater the integration of online activities in the delivery and particularly in the assessment of the course, the greater the participation and interaction online.

There is evidence across all three of these programmes (as well as many other OU courses) that most students welcome the use of new technology – primarily because they see it as contributing to a social climate for learning and to the development of their IT skills. However, the general enthusiasm is tempered by three major drawbacks:

1   The use of computer and communications technologies makes learning at a distance less flexible. Particularly annoying to some students is the

kind of integration of media into core teaching – one of the OU's hall-marks – where after a page or two of print, the student is sent off to listen to a tape, or fire up the computer for a bit of programming, or log-on to the conferencing system. Feedback shows that few students work to the order specified, because it does not suit their study patterns or times. An audio meant to accompany students' first log-on to the conferencing system to talk them through the key strokes and the modem responses, was frequently listened to by students in the car going to work!

2   Asynchronous online interaction is enthusiastically embraced by those who value a 'learning community', but often rejected by those strategic learners who have their eye firmly fixed on the certificate at the end, or who are simply too pressed for time to benefit from such a leisurely and reflective learning medium. Contrary to the expectations of uninitiated users of these systems for actual courses, a common response by students is disappointment at the lack of interaction by their fellow students (and occasionally by their tutor), as the evaluation of MZX records:

> Students reported that their rapport with their tutor developed, and many reported that contact was freer via email than it would have been by telephone. . . . On the other hand, more Internet than conventional students [using face-to-face tutorials] were disappointed in their fellow students, and most felt that there had been insufficient interaction.
>
> (Petre *et al.*, 1997)

3   Attempts by the University to use computer conferencing to substitute for face-to-face meetings have always been resisted by students. On the whole there is agreement (amongst staff and students) that they are different media which must be exploited for their unique possibilities. This conclusion has significant cost implications for the continuance of both face-to-face and electronic support systems. The use of KMi Stadium for lectures and small group tutorials provides a synchronous teaching element and direct contact with tutors, which clearly goes some way to meeting students' perceived needs. In MZX, tutors adapted and exploited the asynchronous systems to fit the situation of running problem solving sessions at a distance. For example, they developed a week-long, asynchronous, role play scenario using problems built up in stages to effect a cumulative, collaborative solution. They also tried mixed-mode tutorials incorporating both email and Internet Relay Chat, backed up by logs and question/answer digests. In the second year of the course, an audiographics (shared whiteboard) system was used for real time tutorials.

The MA benefits from a much stronger online component to the course, and although some students still resist active and interactive participation, comments such as the following show what can be achieved:

For me the benefits of [this online course] could be summarised as being all of those which I would hope that any student would acquire through active engagement in the learning process rather than just passively listening to someone else's ideas. The way in which [this course] was conducted encouraged me to adopt a deep rather than surface approach to my learning. Through both reading and active involvement I was encouraged to link theoretical ideas with practical applications and to articulate my resulting ideas to the rest of the group. The process was challenging, stimulating, interesting and pretty exhausting too! In retrospect I learned more than I thought that I had at the time. In part this happened through the process of reflection, something which cmc seems to me to promote so well, and in part through seeing, reading, absorbing and responding to other people's ideas and perspectives.

(Student on one of IET's online courses)

Another student commenting on the global nature of the learning environment commented: 'I am learning a great deal about myself as a learner in this environment and hopefully will extend this to having more empathy with my fellow learners. It is certainly an eye opener' (MA student).

Faculty views

In 1988, a colleague and I ran an international conference at the Open University about this new medium of computer conferencing. Over 200 people from around the world attended, but despite the offer of free attendance for OU staff, only about half a dozen came. Even course team members of the new OU course which had begun using electronic communication did not all attend. In 1994, I ran a similar conference at the OU which provoked a veritable stampede amongst staff to attend. During that period, the views of the majority went from indifference or disgust with such a use of computer power, to considerable interest and real creativity in applying its potential to their own curriculum and context. The main barrier to extending use is the access problems it creates for students who do not own a machine, and will be put off registering if they are required to buy one. The same applies to further uses of multimedia either on CD-ROM or the Web: faculty are actively investigating the potential for their discipline, but are concerned about raising rather than lowering barriers to entry, which has always been the mission of the University.

Despite considerable interest in a range of new technologies, realism about the advantages of print prevails – both for flexibility and for appropriate delivery of large amounts of discursive text, and no one anticipates 'putting a whole course online'. Even the 'online' second year of IET's Masters Degree uses four set books.

Amongst tutors who work 'at the coal face' interacting with students and marking assignments, there is somewhat less commitment to online activities and the spread of technology. Some are concerned about possible erosion of their jobs, although all the evidence indicates that technologies do not substitute for tutors. On the contrary, if anything, they increase students' demand for tutor contact. More significant is the concern about the increased time it takes to tutor online. In the case of MZX, tutors found this was partially offset by collaborating amongst themselves:

> Re-use and sharing are two crucial means for improving productivity, exploiting expertise, and reducing the load on any one tutor. The increased loads experienced in the early years may well be off-set in subsequent years by the advantages gained in materials collections, re-distributed loads, etc.
>
> (Petre *et al.*, 1997)

As to the global aspect of these programmes, some faculty view the resource and attention dedicated to global expansion as detracting from the support for students and the concern for quality in the home market. Others, particularly those working on global programmes, are enthusiastic. An OBS internal report concludes: 'There are real benefits to staff from cross-cultural working. There is high job satisfaction and in time the experience will be reflected in course design and content' (Open Business School, 1996a).

Senior staff I interviewed all considered that the barriers to further global expansion by the OU were entirely in the minds of staff: their willingness to debate the issues of a global curriculum and to recognise the 'world outside the UK'.

Analysis and conclusions

The image of the OU I have presented here obviously concentrates on its global practice, and readers may be confirmed in their suspicions that the UKOU is set to dominate global education provision, as it has done with distance education in the UK over the past twenty-five years. However, the OU is a large organisation and a very great deal of it is still devoted to doing what it has always done: providing undergraduate education to about 100,000 UK students. My analysis is aimed at assessing the whole institution's capability for delivering education on a global scale.

Benefits from global perspective

While the MA in Open and Distance Education clearly aims to give its students the benefit of a global perspective, both in the use of course material from distance teaching systems around the world and in the collaborative activities amongst students, this course is an exception in the OU curriculum and likely to remain so for some time. It is small, tutored centrally, and uses telecommunications more extensively than any other course in the OU. The vast majority of the OU's non-UK activity has more indirect benefits for students, in terms of a global content or interaction at a global level.

Nevertheless, there is evidence that the exposure of staff to other teaching systems and content, and their experience in adapting and versioning material for other countries, is resulting in somewhat more cross-cultural content on a number of courses. An internal OBS report concludes: 'Much of our material remains highly culture-specific, often gratuitously so. There will need to be considerable editing and modification if our courses are to become more accessible to students from other cultures' (Open Business School, 1996b).

On another level, some of the OU's activities in Eastern Europe and the Middle East have provided a broader perspective to the students there than they would otherwise have been able to acquire. Were we simply contributing to a sense of Western dependence and undermining indigenous attempts to maintain their own culture and practices? One view taken by OU staff is that higher education generally is a 'good thing' which adds value to society. Having a choice of providers is beneficial and therefore exporting it is not a 'bad thing'.

Technology strategy

I think there are a number of very healthy attributes of the OU's technology strategy:

- It is rarely bamboozled by new technologies – at least not past the trial stage. Systems for evaluation and critical appraisal are well established in the organisation and in any case, the numbers of students on courses mean that any technology must be very robust to be applied to live courses. As the Vice-Chancellor has said, 'If we get things wrong, it can mean a lot of hate mail'.
- The size of the organisation means that there are always trials of new or competitive systems taking place and lots of opportunities to try systems in a range of contexts.
- The primary synchronous element in the OU's teaching strategy has always been face-to-face tutorials. As the University globalises, it has begun to build up its expertise in synchronous teaching at a distance using a number of support technologies. On the whole, this does not involve videoconferencing of the lecturing variety, but rather small group tutoring, problem solving, and support sessions.

The OU's approach to distance education would seem to be the ideal model for the educational use of multimedia – large numbers of students on courses which remain the same for several years. In fact, although the courses in this case study do not make extensive use of CD-ROMs, the OU is developing a wide range of CD-ROM material for other courses. Early feedback shows that producing high quality multimedia material is taking too long and costing too much to produce. Of course, this is a common complaint about multimedia, but more experimentation with Web-based systems, with simpler systems and with means of allowing students to produce their own multimedia, are needed to keep in the forefront and to consider global access. Experiments are already in hand with Web CDs whereby the student views the resources on a CD-ROM through a Web browser which in turn can also be used to add an online component where appropriate.

Pedagogical transformation

Despite experience in translating courses, adapting them, working with partners to version material, and collaborating in joint writing, the degree of pedagogical transformation of OU courses for the global market remains very small. The production of courses takes far too long: bureaucratic processes are increasing not decreasing, administrative staff are increasing relative to academic staff, and the course team approach which has served the University well over twenty-five years needs re-thinking in the light of changing demands on the curriculum.

Because of its roots in mass distance education, the OU is probably never going to address the market for leading edge, modular courses with a short life-span. Other providers are better adapted to satisfying this demand. As many futurists and much of the life-long learning literature predict, this will be a large market. The OU may find its global expansion limited by more than the outlook of its staff! The demand for large, relatively undifferentiated products does not figure in many visions of the new global curriculum.

Institutional change

I think the OU's process of institutional change has been extraordinarily successful for a large educational organisation. Perhaps it had less resistance to change than older, more established, universities. Nevertheless, I think the climate of active support for, and eagerness to experiment with, innovative approaches to teaching, is unparalleled in other universities. This is undoubtedly its strongest card in becoming a global educational provider.

Part III

Trends in globalisation

I come now to the most difficult part of the book. It is one thing to raise issues, to research applications and literature, and to interview practitioners and talk to fellow educators. It is another to draw the issues and practice into a coherent view about what is actually happening and what is going to happen. This is what I attempt to do in Part III.

It is well known that futurists and predictors of technology adoption, vastly overestimate the speed of technology take-up, but underestimate the social and psychological impact of the change that technology brings. Doubtless this applies equally to the globalisation of education. I have thus avoided giving date-stamped predictions!

I asked a recent visitor from the Pacific Rim why his very successful training organisation was not offering courses abroad. 'We don't need to sell our courses abroad because there is just so much demand at home,' was his response. He thought that his country was going through an educational transition from reliance on rote learning to a more questioning and reflective approach to learning. We talked about the wider impact of such change: does questioning the content of courses eventually lead to questioning one's elders and one's parents, and hence to the kind of crisis of family and community breakdown which is evident in parts of Western society? This link between a pedagogical approach and the fabric of society more generally, is much too large an issue for me to tackle here, but I mention it simply to reflect the kind of thinking I have discussed with colleagues during my research.

11 Current trends

Overview of case study findings

I have tried to choose applications of global courses in these five case studies which broadly represent current activity in the field. Whether or not they accurately depict general institutional attitudes and educational approaches to global education, we can still draw a number of conclusions from the five studies as independent examples of global education.

First of all, we see that the English language is predominant and that English language providers dominate the field. This comes as no surprise: language is obviously a critical factor on courses in which students from many countries interact, and English is the dominant language in at least two of the most common subjects for global courses: business and information technology. Furthermore, English-speaking countries have dominated the development of the technologies which support global communications. There certainly are examples of cross-border courses in languages other than English: the Scandinavian countries have set up some collaborative ventures; there are some Spanish applications in Latin America; various European countries teach their nationals living in neighbouring countries using technology-based approaches; and French schemes exist amongst Francophone countries. All of these applications are very small at this stage however.

The second conclusion we can draw is that there has been very little real engagement with the cultural issues of global education. I would describe the current approach as careful, surface window dressing. However, I would also add that this is not unexpected at such an early stage. Addressing differences of cultural attitude, educational approach and social outlooks is going to be very challenging. Translating materials into other languages may be necessary, but it is hardly sufficient to tackle the real problem of difference. All of the global practitioners I questioned about this were open in acknowledging that they were only just beginning to take on the challenge of cultural differences. Despite the obvious importance of this issue, the demand from countries for global offerings, and the pressures on providers to expand in global directions, have propelled the innovators into the field. The result, as we see in these case studies, is awareness of the problems and some initial attempts to 'show sensitivity', but few strategies for tackling the fundamental issues – how to give equal voice to local cultures, institutions and educational approaches.

The case studies reflect a third aspect of current trends: diversity. They reflect the whole range from very small scale 'toe in the water' approaches to broad institutional commitment to global development. They show a range of technological approaches to delivery, although I must admit that a satellite TV application would have completed the picture of current trends. My reasons for omitting such a case study are given below. Despite this diversity, the question about global education which many commentators raise is: will the growth of global provision of education lead to diversity of opportunity or to homogenisation and vast global corporations delivering homogenised products? I think we can see both these possibilities in the case studies described here.

Economic globalisation has proceeded at a much faster pace than educational globalisation, by which I mean that people generally are much more aware of their economic interdependence than they are of the advantages and limitations of global education. What we have witnessed at an economic level, despite whatever benefits there may have been, is that one large city looks much the same as another anywhere around the globe and certainly sells most of the same products. Do we see the seeds of the same process taking place in education from the case studies I have presented? After all, the practitioners working at a global level now are the early adopters; the consolidators who follow in their footsteps will, according to the laws of 'diffusion of innovation', be less innovative, less culturally sensitive, less enthusiastic, and less experimental. The IBM, UKOU and JEC case studies give a taste for the kind of large scale global offerings which are possible. There is very clearly an element of homogenisation in the products they offer, because of the scale on which they are operating. The USQ and Duke University applications exemplify the craft level of global provision – small numbers, high tutor/student ratio, hand tooled courses. If these and other types of global offerings are available in increasing numbers and variety, they should provide diversity of opportunity for the individual learner. However, like the 'global city', it seems inevitable that some homogenisation of educational provision will occur from the globalising process. It remains to be seen whether the extra diversity and choice arising from competing global programmes compensates for this.

My fourth conclusion from these case studies is more positive. As with all innovation, one of the main benefits results from the extra attention paid to the process, apart altogether from the changes being made to it. In this context, the attention paid to the learning process, to the role of the teacher, to the skills needed by students, to the institutional support systems, has all been useful in itself. We have seen in all the case studies the way in which the global expansion has been infused with considerations of educational practice, and has caused the whole institution to re-think what it is doing and how it is doing it.

Finally, for all their diversity, the case studies show considerable unanimity about the curriculum areas which define current trends: MBAs and business studies, information technology and computer-related subjects, and open and distance education qualifications, with languages and cultural subjects forming a smaller but, I predict, growing area for the 'second wave'. These topics really reflect the demands of the life-long learning market which currently centres on professional updating, IT skilling and to a lesser extent, leisure concerns.

Technology overview

The case studies also make clear a number of current trends in technology support for global education.

The first trend is a movement away from broadcast or satellite TV as a means of delivering course content. Both the IBM and JEC case studies reflect this trend as a North American phenomenon. The UKOU, which for a very short period in its early planning days was known as the University of the Air because of its association with the BBC, has always used TV programmes as an enrichment to the primary delivery medium of print. The pedagogy which underpins the use of lecture-mode, one-way technologies tends to be teacher-dominated; as we have seen, the educational approach on the ascendancy in Western countries is student-oriented, involving context dependent construction of knowledge through collaborative interaction with materials, the tutor and other students. Most Asian countries and some continental European countries have not, or not yet, adopted these views. Broadcast TV therefore continues to be an appropriate technology in these areas. Where the more interactive technologies are being used (e.g. the Global Executive MBA case study), Asians take longer to adapt to the demands of interactivity and pro-active approaches to collaboration.

Interactivity characterises the second trend. At the most basic level there is simple electronic messaging with the tutor; at the most advanced level there is collaborative activity amongst students particularly where it becomes a significant component of the course content. We begin to see this on the USQ certificate course, in a more developed form on the Global Executive MBA and in an advanced form on the second year of the UKOU Masters degree. All of these examples, however, are small scale. It is still difficult to determine from current trends in global education how these interactive processes can achieve the economics of scale that current trends in higher education and training more generally are beginning to demand. The technology is in place to support the interaction, but the social and educational processes remain in the 'craft phase'.

The third trend – less dominant in global than in national applications – is the use of technology-mediated synchronous events. Operating these on a global scale is always going to be problematic because of the limitations of multiple time zones. The technological 'fix' for this at the moment seems to be Web-casting (either video or audio only), which can be attended 'live', slightly delayed, or any time thereafter as the material is stored on the host Web site. I predict that these real or nearly real time events will become standard practice on global courses, for student interactions on small courses, and for tutor and guest lecturer presentations with some student interaction on large courses.

One technology solution

I have tried to show, both through discussion of issues arising from global education, and specific examples in the case studies, that technology is only one component of a successful programme, whether global or not. The corollary to this is that no one technology will be *the* solution to global education. Daniel points out the dangers of an institution putting all its 'technology eggs in one basket' (Daniel, 1996, p. 146). Nevertheless, I think it is a fair conclusion to draw from these case studies that the Web is a major force in the globalisation of education. This is different from concluding that it is a 'one stop shopping' solution to education, although many vendors of software interfaces are trying to do just that. It is still a medium in its frontier stage of development – full of potential promise and actual rubbish! What accounts for the Web's success as the most rapidly emerging communications technology ever are two factors important for global delivery:

- the standardised format, whereby the hypertext transfer protocol (http) will open a homepage anywhere in the world;
- simplicity of use, integrating and providing access to earlier services which were much more complicated to learn to use.

While one case study programme (USQ) was carried out entirely on the Web (apart from some reading material), most use it as one element in the whole course delivery. For this reason, and because the medium is so new, it is too early to say what cognitive effects the Web is having on learners. Most feedback shows that students enjoy the Web: they welcome the choice of routes it offers and the flexibility and ease of access. Until there is sustained use of hypermedia for whole degree programmes and little supplementing with other, more narrative media, it will be difficult to determine whether the Web has detrimental (or positive) effects on learning.

None of the case studies I presented uses the full range of Web facilities already being applied on courses at national or local level (see Khan, 1997 for examples). Part of the reason for the relatively 'low-tech' uses of the Web on global courses obviously is access limitations. The Duke University programme shows the most adventurous uses because it controlled the students' hardware and software. Another part of the reason may be the well-known warning against experimenting on two fronts at the same time – global delivery and innovative technology. Nevertheless, to varying degrees the case studies include the following course delivery and support mechanisms:

- assessment systems: self-assessment questions, tests and examinations using cgi scripts (the UKOU);
- research facilities: through search engines, online journals and communications with other researchers (all examples);
- multimedia capabilities: text, graphics, audio, video, animations (Global Executive MBA);
- integrated communications: interactive discussions and collaborative activities (all examples except JEC);
- electronic publishing: students can present their work through the Web for comment by the teacher and other students (UKOU MA);
- synchronous and asynchronous access: to course materials and to discussion (Global Executive MBA and UKOU KMi Stadium);
- ease of updating: changes to Web pages for adding topical material, updating Web references (all examples).

Can we predict from these case studies that the Web will dominate global provision to the exclusion of other technologies? I think not. Print still forms a significant component even of the so-called Web courses. Face-to-face meetings also are still clung to as important components of the learning process, particularly in some curriculum areas (e.g. the soft subjects). Videoconferencing, whether by ISDN or satellite, or combinations of both, is not a dead-end technology. There are good uses of it – albeit mainly in the training sector – which will guarantee its place in the delivery media options independent of the Web. Stand-alone uses of the computer, although not particularly significant in these case studies, will continue to provide richer multimedia experiences for some time to come than will be possible over a network. Using the Web to update and view CD-ROM material will certainly become increasingly common, and perhaps the same kind of approach will be used eventually to deliver the kind of video and audio teaching material currently provided on cassettes.

Trends from other providers

In order to expand this view of current trends, we need to examine a number of other providers who are either in too early a phase to be appropriate for full case studies or are not yet operating on a global scale.

Joint course development

The first one I will examine is that of joint course development, an approach to global education which I have mentioned in earlier chapters but which did not feature strongly in any of the case studies.

The European Commission has over the last eight years or so funded a variety of projects which set out to produce jointly written courses at a transnational level. A number of reports have been prepared on the difficulties involved and the technologies which can support joint development. While transnational course development is hardly a European concept either in origin or exclusive practice, it is particularly appropriate to the European context in which many small bordering countries with different languages and cultures have similar needs in education and training. By collaboratively producing courses, it is hoped, the 'exporting model' of global education whereby one institution sells its products in other markets, can be avoided. Telecommunications technologies are used to support a transnational course team exchanging draft materials, discussing course issues, and managing the editing and commenting processes. Each participating institution then delivers the whole programme to their own students, with cross-border communications amongst students as an optional enrichment. Students benefit from an international perspective primarily through the course materials (and perhaps secondarily through interactions with students at other institutions taking the same course). Academics and course developers at each participating institution have a sense of ownership of the course, thus avoiding the problem of 'not invented here' which inevitably accompanies courses imported from another institution, particularly a foreign one. In theory at least, sharing the development costs and reducing the number of staff from any one institution involved in producing the course, should be an efficient and economical way for each institution to increase its course offerings. It is easy to see why joint course development has become almost a Holy Grail – devoutly to be desired but so difficult to achieve.

The difficulties of producing courses in this way are really an amplification of the same problems which course teams within a single institution face in developing courses: different personal agendas, different views of the subject matter, different approaches to teaching and learning, different styles of writing and different tolerances to criticism from colleagues. With cross-institutional course teams, these differences will probably be greater, and with cross-cultural course teams, these differences may even be unbridgable. The UKOU has been using the course team approach to developing courses for twenty-five years – as have many other distance teaching organisations. There is evidence that when the team 'gels', the process of joint development works positively in producing a course of very high quality. For many of the reasons outlined above, the course team process can lead to acrimony amongst members and the resulting course becomes more an amalgam of disparate bits. Most of the academics I interviewed who had taken part in joint course development with colleagues outside their own country had found the experience fairly bruising. Nevertheless, many people – both practitioners and policy makers (in the European Commission) – see this as the model to which to aspire.

One of the joint course developments which the Commission is sponsoring currently involves the area of technology management, a subject which benefits from international perspectives. The course team consists of five partners (universities, training organisations and unions) across a number of countries of Europe. The team plans to use ISDN videoconferencing for some group meetings, and Lotus Notes as the medium for exchanging drafts and discussing progress. The aim is to produce two courses which each participating member will tutor and accredit from their own institutional base. The content will be stored digitally and each institution will print just what they require at any one time; students will use the Internet for assignments and tutor contact, and for real time events. I asked one of the participating course developers what he hoped to gain from this process, knowing that some of his colleagues had found similar activities very difficult in the past. He was most positive about the advantages for students:

- a wider perspective of the subject than a course produced by a single institution;
- a de-packaged course which will demand more initiative on the part of the student to make sense of the whole content;
- a more acceptable alternative to the 'export model' of transnational education.

Another example comes from two Veterinary Schools at universities in Australia (Walsh, 1997). Using the Web as a vehicle for delivering the jointly developed course, the two schools also wanted their students to interact across sites, so videoconferencing and email were introduced. Walsh lists some of the problems they encountered in the joint development process: differing teaching strategies of the two institutions, differing priorities of each faculty, and varied timing for the use of course materials (causing problems for telecommunications between students taking the course during the same semester). Despite poor take-up of the electronic communications, Walsh notes the following advantages of the first presentation:

> While the students responded positively to the technology, they also valued the stimulation of breaking the traditional isolation of Australian veterinary students by working with their peers from across the continent. Faculty found that the need for different specialists to collaborate catalysed the development of seamless integrated course materials and gave them insight into their teaching.
>
> (Walsh, 1997, p. 101)

I think we will see more examples of this approach to global education, but because of the social, cultural and personal hurdles of joint course development, I do not anticipate that it will become a dominant mode, unfortunately.

Individualised learning

The second trend which is emerging from some of the very latest examples of global learning providers is methods for facilitating and supporting individualised learning. I describe the approach of two practitioners here, the first is Deutsche Telekom and the second is Waite Group Press.

In early 1997, Deutsche Telekom (DT) launched its Global Learning range of services, which has developed from a realisation that today's telecommunications companies are no longer simply carriers but intelligent purveyors of information. DT's brochure launching the new programme states that as a future-oriented telecommunications company, they have got to provide more than just an optimised technical infrastructure for online services. Deutsche Telekom must also offer multimedia solutions and services from a single source, organise content, and help present it in user-friendly forms.

One of the targets they are aiming at is 'individualised learning'. They note that internal training and development is moving away from the use of training centres towards individual, network-based methods which offer the trainee more choice, flexibility and personal feedback from the tutor. Working through partner providers, they intend to offer the following three methods of individual learning.

- CBT and multimedia applications for employees of one company using the system are accessible through Global Learning; a tutor is available for email questions and correcting homework, and through a 'testing room', the trainee can take the exam at any time of the day or night.
- Siemens Nixdorf are using Global Learning to offer training both to their own employees and to other companies. The special emphasis is on goal-oriented training in which the trainees can define at the start of the process what goals they want to achieve. Self-testing allows them to test, rate and document their own progress. Teletutors provide assistance via email or by directly linking in to the students' on-screen work. In future, up to eight student locations will be connectable via ISDN to create a virtual classroom.
- The Global Learning Institute is a learning and consultation forum, whereby professional consulting will be available on how to transfer conventional basic training and further training to new learning systems (e.g. Intranets), how to train tutors, course developers and administrators. The Institute will have a virtual faculty consisting of experts from around the world, pooling their expertise to provide individual answers to queries, small tailored courses, and introductory seminars.

Most of their offerings are still in the planning stages, but the direction and the approach are both in place. I have only highlighted a few of the wide-ranging elements of Global Learning; some of the others have a Germany-specific focus, some are aimed at schools, and others have a definite global spread. One commentator describes it as, 'much more impressive than anything done by any other PTT, in Europe or indeed elsewhere' (Bacsich, 1997b).

Waite Group Press provides an example of the way in which publishers are using the Web to enhance or in some cases replace printed books. In this particular case, Waite Group Press uses the Web to enhance their books on computers by including with the purchase access to online tutorials and activities. Called 'intelligent books', this full sequence of programmed exercises takes the learner from novice stage to complete mastery. More details can be seen at their Web site: http://www.mcp.com/waite/ezone.

As with Deutsche Telekom, we see in this example business sectors which once supported educational institutions, now competing with them to meet the demand for individualised and life-long learning.

Online support systems

A third trend in online education is the development of interfaces or shells, usually Web-based, to support and integrate all of the components of distance education provision. I describe here one example arising from the university community and one from the business sector.

Virtual-U is a Web-based learning environment which integrates the facilities to support course design and presentation, tutorial and collaborative learning activities, and administrative and assessment arrangements. Designed by academics at Simon Fraser University, it uses the common device of a visual metaphor of the physical campus, with buildings entitled library, admin, courses, cafe, gallery, etc. to help the student to navigate through the key facilities offered by the interface. On the course support side, the system offers the course author a template for preparing the syllabus and another for designing the conference structure for online collaboration and communication (Harasim *et al.*, 1997). Frameworks such as this one are always evolving as new versions of Web browsers emerge, new facilities such as frames and Java become available, and feedback from students contributes to the refinement of the system.

Another more comprehensive system has been designed by Real Education, a small US company, which claims to have produced the first complete online university for University of Colorado (although this claim has been disputed by the distance education community). Called CU Online, the system boasts that it provides the same range of services a traditional student can get on campus. This includes: audio, animated graphics, real time discussion, asynchronous discussion, audio and video email attachments, automatic testing, a library with over 1,400 newspapers, Web-based discussion threads, an online catalogue, registration, admission, academic counselling, career counselling and student union. Real Education's Rob Helmick says:

> Our mission is to build and manage complete online university campuses and continuing education centers for our clients. Our goal is to affiliate with clients that are major universities, community college consortiums, corporations looking to create corporate universities and major continuing

education providers. . . . Real Education is constantly striving to build the
highest quality online educational delivery system.

(http://www.realeducation.com)

From the students' point of view, this integration offers the convenience of
one interface for access to teaching, interaction and administrative support.
From the academics' point of view, the templates and support tools obviate
the need to learn HTML, and provide guidance in moving their teaching into
a new medium. Neither of these examples operates globally, but it is easy to
see this kind of service being central to an organisation which is global, even
when the administrative and tutorial queries are answered by a local partner.

Migrating to the Web

My fourth trend has been emphasised over and over again throughout this
book, but this example provides another angle on the 'great Web debate', from
a global provider which can hardly be overlooked.

MOLI is Microsoft's framework for offering its third party training
providers a vehicle for online training courses in Microsoft products. As with
the CU Online and Deutsche Telekom frameworks, it provides facilities for
presentation, interaction and administration of courses. It was originally
developed on a proprietary Microsoft system, but this has been discontinued
in favour of the new Web version. It now provides interactive quizzes, and live
video chats using whiteboards (Microsoft's NetMeeting and NetShow). Like
the Global Learning model, Microsoft uses higher education institutions and
training partners to provide the course content and the tutoring. These
providers use other media to deliver course content in some instances (e.g.
print and CD-ROM).

Feedback from the roughly 6,000 students in the system currently, indicates
a move away from real time group chat as a useful learning mode in favour of
real time presentations with graphics and audio by the tutor, since students
can view them at their convenience and replay many times. Sometimes whiteboard collaborative sessions are held in which each student can speak, hear
the other students, and draw diagrams on a shared screen. The majority of
students are IT professionals, often independent contractors needing just-
in-time job improvement skills. About 35 per cent are certification candidates
preparing for exams and about 10 per cent are people wanting to improve
their IT skills for better performance on their present job. While the training
providers in the UK and US do accept students located in other countries, and
they anticipate this side of their business growing, by far the majority of their
students are located in the same country.

I asked my Microsoft interviewee what the company's view was of the
future of the Web:

We say 'the Web is the Way' for education, training and technical certification testing. The advent of the Intranet now provides unlimited access to businesses, and the continuing rise of Web use internationally allows enormous accessibility worldwide. Microsoft is totally committed to the Web. Wider bandwidth at every level, better compression for code and media, better speed of connection, better routing speed, and better traffic capacities are coming. It is improving daily and will be quite adequate for full multimedia training with live instruction within two years.

(Personal communication, April 1997)

Microsoft knows that technology is not the central factor in successful education, as even poor technology succeeds in the presence of great design and good human interaction. Nevertheless, this migration from a proprietary system to the Web must be seen as significant. When the giant of the industry rolls over, it is as well for the rest of us to be on the right side of the bed!

Conclusions

I have presented what I see as the obvious trends in global education which are visible now in the activities of current practitioners. Naturally I am more confident of my conclusions in this chapter than I am of those in the next chapter where I speculate on future trends. Even so, there are areas of provision (videoconferencing, CD-ROM-based teaching), types of technologies (cable, mobile communications) and emerging providers (university consortia and for profit providers) which I have not covered in as much detail as they deserve. Furthermore, I have not been able to obtain access to evaluation data in quite the depth I would have liked. I have had to strike a balance between comprehensiveness and timeliness.

12 Future trends

Central issues of global education

As I try to draw together the disparate themes of this book, I find they coalesce around three issues which are, of course, interrelated. I have looked at them from several angles throughout the preceding chapters, either at a general level in the first part, or at the application level in the second part. In this final chapter, I address these three critical issues directly and give my own views.

The three issues which I think will most critically affect the nature and growth of global education are:

- the future transformation of universities;
- the cultural and social impact of global education;
- the educational exploitation of computer and communications technologies.

I have no doubt that global education will continue to grow, but there are many forms of the phenomenon, as I hope I have shown. Some are very much more to be desired than others, and the three issues I have identified here will, I think, determine which types of global education come to dominate the field.

The future of the university

Discussions about the shape of the university in the future are widespread in the educational press; they preoccupy the higher education policy decision makers of governments and even the talk amongst academic staff. Papers on the subject appear regularly on the Web and academic conferences devoted to the issue are common events. In the melting pot is the whole traditional university mould, and whatever new designs eventually emerge, global expansion will be more rather than less evident. I say this because most of the commentary I read about solutions or directions for universities centres on a move away from lectures as the only or primary teaching method towards resource-based approaches which de-couple the content from the teaching support. Although the videoconferencing mode of global education is one application to the contrary, my view is that the dominant systems even now, and certainly in the future, rely on pre-preparation of the content (CD-ROM, the Web, print, CBT) and a mixture of delivery technologies to provide support and guidance.

The history of global education, while not as venerable as that of universities, is steeped in a colonial, paper-based, niche tradition, and is now emerging into a technology-based major phenomenon. As with all consumer demands, if the traditional provider ignores the demand (i.e. universities), others will quickly appear to meet it. I have described in some detail, the range of other educational providers which have already appeared in response to the un-met demands for education and training: private for-profit universities, virtual universities, corporate universities, and educational brokers. The major concern about this development is the consummerisation of education which drives many of these new institutions. The focus of a business is profit; the focus of a university is knowledge.

> These companies are in the knowledge business – knowledge for profit – and they are revolutionizing the way we learn at the same time as they are creating a powerful new opportunity for growth in business. . . . Behind it all looms a gargantuan government-run education system incapable of handling a doubling of knowledge about every seven years. The knowledge revolution will power the new global economy, reshape many of our institutions – particularly education – and touch every aspect of our lives. Business sees the opportunity, and it is driving ahead full speed to realize this vision to adapt to, and profit from, the realities of the new informational economy.
>
> (Davis and Botkin, 1995, pp. 14–15)

So we have, on the one hand, the reality of competition which is undercutting the university both at home and abroad, and on the other, the belief that entering the global market is cheapening and ultimately undermining the whole notion of a university.

The case studies in the second part of this book have shown one way out of this dilemma: collaboration. It is not an easy, nor a new solution. It can take a number of forms:

- working with a complementary partner, such as a network provider, which has a different core business, but one that is essential to the globalisation of education;
- working with an educational partner abroad, which has local knowledge but needs more content and a greater range of courses than it can produce locally;
- working with a consortia of universities in which each partner supplies some courses, but has access to all;

- working with international partners to develop courses jointly.

As we have seen throughout the book, diversity is the watchword of the new educational provision. Entering the global market an institution may choose to work in all four of these (and other) modes. One member of senior academic staff I spoke with said that his university would soon have both competitive and collaborative relationships with the same partner either in different countries or in different curriculum areas.

Another way of facing the dilemma is a rigorous re-thinking of:

- the curriculum (its length, content, relevance);
- the delivery of it (asynchronous, technology-based, interactive);
- the educational approach (constructivist, collaborative, student-centred).

This is an educational interpretation of the standard business process of re-engineering. This would involve rationalising and quantifying teaching to produce higher customer satisfaction, and is not the right approach. As Porter (1993) argues, this kind of re-engineering should be applied only to administrative processes in higher education.

Brown and Duguid (1995) describe the university's unique heritage as a 'complex relationship between knowledge, communities, and credentials'. When these three elements are kept in mind, I think universities can become global providers without losing their morals or their quality. In fact, through the processes of re-thinking and refining what they do, I predict that in some sectors there will be improvements due to global practice. The role of the teacher, transformed into a guide through the undifferentiated materials on the Web; the ability of virtual communities to build on global perspectives; and the opportunity to re-design credentials to reflect mastery rather than memorisation, all offer possibilities more interesting than remaining with the status quo. In short, global education is not inherently immoral, consumerist, or sub-standard. It all depends on the attitude and approach which the provider adopts to the practice.

My guess is that a number of prestige universities will restructure in the direction of global education, and this will give more credence to a wide range of other universities to enter behind them. Eventually the practice will be accepted as the legitimate domain of universities. Many forms of global courses will be tried for some time to come, as expertise builds, consortia work together in producing courses, and the technologies which deliver them develop. Examples of the current diversity of forms are:

- satellite delivered lecturing to several sites with medium-sized numbers;
- small Web-based courses;
- print-based courses with electronic support systems to relatively large numbers;

- multiple media courses, combining a range of synchronous and asynchronous media;
- TV-based materials with various forms of tutor support.

Ten years from now, more or less, I suspect that two or three forms will emerge as the most successful and will dominate the stage, though not to the total exclusion of the others. The same range between small elite providers and mass providers which exists now at a national level will be reflected at the global level. However, the extent to which universities partake in this growth, or become the 'hacks' for commercial providers, will depend on how universities come through the transition period currently dominating their development. 'Reform without change', says Goodman, would be the worst option in that old practices would simply be adapted to new media (Goodman, 1995). If the challenge to improve university practice is really grasped, students both at home and abroad will be the beneficiaries. Brown and Duguid (1995) believe that 'the university's oversight and credentialling function will still be needed in the digital age, and so will the learner's need for access to communities of scholars'. It is merely the relationship between these which must change.

I can see the emergence of global degrees, by which I mean degrees awarded by virtual consortia of universities and other providers. Just as in the economic sector, global businesses are transcending national groupings in favour of sectors of interest which completely ignore national boundaries, so I suspect global education will eventually develop along curricula lines. In this way, it will ignore national regulations and limitations which currently exist around the issue of credentialling. In fact, we see this transnational grouping at the research level where academics, using the Internet, work more closely with colleagues in their field all over the world, than with academics down the corridor of their own institution.

The current debate about the future of the university has, on the one hand, those predicting its demise as outmoded, elitist, and unwilling to adapt, and on the one hand, those who point out that universities have survived great social and technological change for over 500 years and will ride out current upheavals more or less intact. My research leads me to predict incremental changes to universities, some rapid and some fundamental. Closures and amalgamations seem unavoidable, and purely campus-based institutions will become a small and marginalised sector, while international and global institutions, consortia and new providers will dominate the education and training market for life-long learning and professional training and updating. The undergraduate market will be the last to evolve.

Cultural and social impact of global education

Many pious words are uttered about the advantages of education in bringing us together into a global village, sensitive to the differences amongst cultures, respecting the viewpoints of all participants on a course regardless of their background or country of origin. Indeed, I have added to them throughout these pages myself. But what are the chances that global education will do anything of the sort? What will prevent the exact opposite – namely, that prejudice, domination and rejection will result from further exposure to our global classmates? Gayol sees these two possibilities as opposing forces:

> In the globalization era, there are two main cultural forces: integrationism and segregationism. The first refers to the homogenization of general values, behaviors and perspectives, the second to the particularism and differentiation of small groups. These are centrifugal and centripetal forces, respectively.
>
> (Gayol, 1996, p. 82)

The primary influences on how we negotiate which of these will be the dominant force in any sustained period are family, environment, media and education. It is the latter which usually has the weakest impact.

> Education may have only a small influence on individual and social experience, but it is the only arena in which to think about the consequences . . . to discuss and decide what should be shared, what should be changed, and what should be kept of our cultural backgrounds.
>
> (*ibid.*)

In this sense global educators have an opportunity and a duty to counteract the influences of the entertainment industry and consumer patterns. It will not happen without intent, however. I have on my shelves two academic books called, respectively, *History of Art and Music*, and *World Study of History*. While both have an introductory chapter on China, essentially they are histories of the Western world. The problem is not so much the content as the titles! Another aspect of Western domination is highlighted by Moore, whose concern centres on the spread of Western consumerist mentality into cultures which have always been community oriented: 'As we enter into educational interactions with individuals and nations outside the Atlantic culture, we have to consider if and how our programs might corrupt their culture with our consumerism' (Moore, 1996, p. 193).

However, we have seen in the case study section of the book that even when providers want to play the post-imperial international role, they face an uphill struggle. I am reminded of an incident relayed to me by a friend. He decided to do something about his garden which was completely overgrown with weeds. In fact, there was only one flower, a daffodil, worth preserving. He set out with enthusiasm and lots of tools. By the end of the day, he had managed to sever the flower off the daffodil and cut through the daffodil bulb. So, too, good intentions in cultural interactions are not enough. Many educators are entering the global garden with similar naïveté and good will, but without an understanding of the power of their tools to damage what is actually very delicate – the culture and society of a country struggling to survive against global influences.

I observe that the most thoughtful practitioners of global education advocate beginning in areas of the curriculum which have a global content. In this way, all participants have an equal status and an equal contribution to make; for example, global business practice, studies of foreign cultures, and second language learning.

Trans-border consortia, where each partner contributes courses to the pool, are another way of avoiding the trap of the dominant provider and the dependent receiver. Buyers of educational products should be sellers as well. These consortia are, sadly, not very common as yet. One of the main drawbacks is resolving the copyright issues on such courses.

A third approach to the problem of cultural domination is to focus not on exporting courses at all, but on the contrary, on developing resources and international contacts to enable one's own students to become global citizens. I have already described one example of this in the form of joint course development in the previous chapter. Alexander and Blight (1996) outline a range of ways in which Australian educators should overcome their geographic isolation and enter the global education field. Some of their suggestions include:

- producing materials about Australia (e.g. CD-ROMs) for use by other countries;
- setting up online interactions and structured collaborative activities with students studying similar courses in other countries;
- using information technology to provide opportunities for vicarious travel;
- participating in online international conferences;
- using multimedia technology to give students experience and language teaching from other countries.

As the authors explain:

> The debate about the globalisation of higher education with its overtones of intellectual and cultural imperialism has overshadowed the potential for internationalisation of education. While there may be something to fear from globalisation, information and communication technologies have many potential positive benefits to bring in the internationalisation of higher education. A distinction is drawn between internationalisation and globalisation. Internationalisation is about nations and interchange between nations, in our case in the area of higher education. Globalisation involves a supranationalism that ignores national boundaries, ignoring the wishes of nations in respect of higher education.
>
> (Alexander and Blight, 1996, p. 66)

In short, they are arguing for the use of information technology to internationalise the curriculum and to provide opportunities for students to interact with their peers in other countries. This approach obviously separates the believers in true globalism from those who would make a profit from it. And much work of the kind they advocate is already taking place. Furthermore, I think this work will go a long way towards laying firm foundations for global education in the export sense of the word – building up the kind of expertise in working with educators in other countries, in handling cultural sensitivities and in understanding more about other countries, which are all necessary to running global courses with more than good intent. However, Alexander and Blight want to see this international model as a substitute for the export model, not as an alternative or as a precursor, regarding the current free trade in education as an educational invasion. My analysis of the situation is that the forces driving global education and the demand from many countries for it, is too strong to be resisted. We must find ways of globalising without colonising.

Lundin, another Australian concerned about the ethics and cultural implications of global education, looks to the development of a 'third culture' due to the increase of cross-cultural communications as a possible approach. He cites media researchers who see a third culture being constructed when materials from one culture are studied by people in a different culture. Material from both the interacting cultures is used to fill locally and temporally defined functions outside both cultures but intelligible to participants from both who are involved in the particular interaction (Lundin, 1996). Educators should certainly consult the literature on cross cultural media research as a first step in developing material which teaches without imposing a cultural perspective.

One study of global media and their possible effect on education points out that entertainment crosses cultural borders much more easily than education (Cunningham *et al.*, 1997). Just as it is much more complex to teach someone than to entertain them, so it is even more complex to do this across cultural and language barriers.

Educational use of new technology

Futurists are fond of looking back at previous so-called educational revolutions in order to disparage the hype about current innovations. The overselling of most educational technology is really laughable, if it were not such an indictment of our ability to learn from past mistakes. One can only conclude that education is a schizophrenic process: both wanting change, even revolution, yet resisting it and even sabotaging it. The current revolutionary possibility centres on the Web. I have no doubt that even this phenomenally successful medium will soon be seen to have been oversold as an educational tool, and it will take its place in the toolkit of teachers and course designers as one of many technologies to consider and to use in particular contexts. One of those contexts will undoubtedly be global education. The Web still attracts the most innovative course re-engineers, software designers and teachers working at the coal face with students. The trick is to concentrate on the innovations they are effecting, not on the technology which happens to be underlying it at the moment.

What these innovations point to is a new role for the teacher, for the student and for course material. It centres on the construction of knowledge by the student, using resources like the Web and a teacher as facilitator, to 'wrestle with the challenge of knowledge construction [which] is essential for the learning process' (Yang, 1996). Yang goes on to characterise the role of course developers as that of empowering learners 'to actively construct their knowledge through linking, annotating, and other activities to achieve the full potential of hypermedia systems' (Yang, 1996, p. 47).

Information is no longer something to organise, transmit and memorise, but something to work with, think with, discuss, negotiate and debate with partners.

Are students prepared for this change? Obviously many are, as demographic data shows a huge rise in home use of the Web, even among non-traditional populations (personal correspondence with Microsoft, April 1997). My own experience with Open University students is that just as many are *not* ready. In a study of students on a course delivered through CD-ROM and Internet resources, our research (Macdonald and Mason, 1997) found about a third who were enthusiastic, with comments like: 'I enjoyed this approach and liked the independence', and 'It's when you do something practical, that you really learn how to do it'. But at least a third were overwhelmed by the information, the extra work entailed in coping with this and their lack of time to deal with it: 'It didn't suit me at all. . . . I don't have time to cope with ambiguities', and 'Choice is a good thing for people who have time to follow up the leads'.

My research leads me to believe that there is much talk about what technology can do and how much the teaching role must change, and even about the demand from students for this change, but little evidence of fundamental change:

> Many of the next generation of students will be very different. They will be increasingly empowered and aware consumers. They will have a choice of educational products, made available internationally. They will expect technical sophistication. Many young people are growing up in a world in which they communicate with, and through, computers, and they experience the world on sophisticated screens. Soon, they will live in a world of multimedia, and expect the same of their education.
>
> (Pritchard, 1995)

While I don't dispute any of this, I would argue that most students are not prepared for the need to take on the responsibility for directing their own learning, for pacing and motivating themselves, for managing and using the information available, and for constructing the knowledge, which previously the lecturer carried out for them. It is to all the skills of learning how to learn that we as educators need to turn our attention, in order that the transformation of the university, the cultural impact of global education and the empowerment which technology promises take place in a positive rather than negative way.

The Web is the archetypal medium of choice and transfer of initiative to the learner. Romiszowski compares Web choice to multi-channel digital television:

> If today the typical USA resident regularly uses only four or five out of the forty or fifty channels that are piped to the household, what may be the position some years down the line when 500 channels are available in every house? And if a proportion of the channels is made available either for education or public access information distribution as opposed to entertainment, what is the likelihood that, if people choose to access these channels, they will benefit as much as they hoped to in terms of identifying useful information, understanding it, and learning how to use it in practice?
>
> (Romiszowski, 1997, p. 31)

There is absolutely no evidence that learners are able or willing to do without teachers, no matter how well designed the materials, how extensive the resources or how 'just-in-time' the learning is accessible. The fundamental role of the teacher or tutor has not changed, but the mode of operation has and will continue to require re-conceptualising.

I predict that the increasing diversity of educational opportunities represented by digital TV and the Web will lead to the growth of a new educational role: a sort of super-tutor who knows what resources, courses and information sources are available in a particular area, and helps the average citizen to navigate through networks, identifying the materials worth attending to and those to ignore, recommending a personal learning plan including courses as well as other 'learning bytes', and advising on the most appropriate mentors. Just as people have personal fitness trainers, so they will have personal learning trainers.

Alternative responses to the global challenge

How do the practitioners of global education regard what they are doing? Are they crass consumerists, lingering imperialists and technology freaks? I certainly encountered no one in any of these categories; all were committed to educational principles. Nevertheless, there were differences in their outlook and response to the global challenge. Amongst the global providers and would-be providers I have interviewed, I notice one of three approaches to the process:

1   The most common I would caricature as 'holier than thou': convinced of the value of global education and their mission to carry it out. Enthusiasm for the benefits of communication technologies is often part of the package.
2   A second approach I would typify as grim determination: 'we can't be left out of this process; it's a fight for survival'. The driving force here is fear, and the reaction to the necessary evil which global education represents to them is to swallow their belief in an ideal model of education while mimicking it with vastly reduced resources.
3   A timid churchmouse is my image of the third approach to globalisation, which usually involves very small scale projects, usually initiated by some outside chance or relationship, and usually adopted very soberly.

These descriptions are not intended critically, but are made simply by way of observation and as part of my efforts to document these early steps in global education. To complete the picture, I give my own views as author in the final section.

A personal response

I began researching and thinking about global education a few years ago with a clear idea in my mind about what it constituted and what the advantages were. I set out to find examples of institutions and course designers and teachers who were practising the model of global teaching I had in mind; namely, electronically delivered courses to students in many countries. What I found was much greater diversity than I had imagined: in educational providers, in types of provision, and in reasons for doing it. I hope I have conveyed some of this richness in the preceding chapters.

My own experience of designing and tutoring online courses with students from many countries has always been a positive one – I find the concept exciting and educationally worthwhile. Now, with wider knowledge of other people's experience, and other applications, both large scale and small, I see the whole process as very much more challenging, with many more pitfalls and inherent limitations than I originally envisaged. I am no less committed, but a lot more aware of the dangers.

Designing, tutoring and managing global programmes is a high risk enterprise. It takes talented staff at all levels, unwavering support from the host institution and a real commitment to student learning, in order to produce a high quality course. As I embark on tutoring a course I have been involved in designing for a global market, I am still excited about the opportunities – and watching out for daffodil flowers and bulbs!

Bibliography

Alexander, S. and Blight, D. (1996) 'Internationalisation of Education through the Virtual University' in G. Hart and J. Mason (eds) *The Virtual University?*, Symposium Proceedings and Case Studies, University of Melbourne.

Allen, A. (1993) 'Culture as a Learning Variable: Implications for Quality Assurance in Distance Education' in A. Tait (ed.) *Conference Papers: Quality Assurance in Open and Distance Learning*, pp. 7–24, Cambridge: Open University East Anglian Region.

Amos, P. (1997) quoted in *Rocky Mountain News*, Business Section, 31 January.

Anderson, T. and Mason, R. (1993) 'International Computer Conferencing for Professional Development: The Bangkok Project', *The American Journal of Distance Education*, vol. 7, no. 2, pp. 5–18.

Bacsich, P. (1997a) 'Virtual Universities', *Learning in a Global Information Society*, LearnTel, Issue 12.

—— (1997b) 'Deutsche Telekom Launches Global Learning', *Learning in a Global Information Society*, LearnTel, Issue 12.

Barnett, L., Brunner, D., Maier, P. and Warren, A. (1996) *Technology in Teaching and Learning*, Interactive Learning Centre, University of Southampton.

Bates, A. (1995) *Technology, Open Learning and Distance Education*, London: Routledge.

Bennett, E. (1996) 'Computer Mediated Communication, T102 and Retention', PLUM Paper No. 76, Milton Keynes: Institute of Educational Technology, The Open University.

Berge, Z. (1997) 'Characteristics of Online Teaching in Post-Secondary Formal Education', http://star.ucc.nau.edu/~mauri/moderate/onteach.html.

Birkerts, S. (1994) *The Gutenberg Elegies. The Fate of Reading in an Electronic Age*, New York: Fawcett Columbine.

Bos, E., Kikstra, A. and Morgan, C. (1996) 'Multiple Levels of Use of the Web as a Learning Tool' in *Educational Telecommunications, 1996*, proceedings of ED-TELECOM, Association for the Advancement of Computing in Education, Charlottesville, VA.

Brown, J. S. and Duguid, P. (1995) 'Universities in the Digital Age', Xerox Palo Alto Research Paper, July, Palo Alto, CA.

Burge, E. and Roberts, J. (1993) 'Classrooms with a Difference. A Practical Guide to the Use of Conferencing Technologies', Toronto: Ontario Institute for Studies in Education.

Collins, M. and Berge, Z. (1996) 'Student Evaluation of Computer Conferencing in a

(Primarily) Audioconferencing Distance Learning Course' in M. Thompson (ed.) *Internationalism in Distance Education: A Vision for Higher Education*, ACSDE Research Monograph No. 10, Pennsylvania State University, PA.

Collis, B. (1996) *Tele-Learning in a Digital World: the Future of Distance Learning*, London: International Thomson Computer Press.

Corrigan, D. (1996) *The Internet University. College Courses by Computer*, Harwich, MA: Cape Software Press.

Cunningham, S., Tapsall, S., Ryan, Y., Stedman, L., Bagdon, K. and Flew, T. (1997) 'New Media and Borderless Education', Canberra: Department of Employment, Education, Training and Youth Affairs, Higher Education Division, Evaluations and Investigations Program.

Daniel, J. (1996) *Mega-Universities and Knowledge Media*, London: Kogan Page.

Davis, S. and Botkin, J. (1995) *The Monster Under the Bed: How Business is Mastering the Opportunity of Knowledge for Profit*, New York: Simon and Schuster.

Deutsche Telekom (1996) 'Continuing Education with a Star', *Vision*, 5, pp. 56–7.

Dewar, T. (1996) 'Adult Learning Online', http://www.cybercorp.net/~tammy/lo/oned2.html.

Durham, T. (1996) 'Cable links TV to Net', *Times Higher Education Supplement*, September.

Edwards, R. (1995) 'Different Discourses, Discourses of Difference: Globalisation, Distance Education and Open Learning', *Distance Education*, vol. 16, no. 2.

Ehrmann, S. (1991) 'Gauging the Educational Value of a College's Investments in Technology', *Educom Review*, XXVI: 3, 4, pp. 24–8.

—— (1994) 'Responding to the Triple Challenge Facing Post-Secondary Eduction: Accessibility, Quality, Costs. A Report for the Organisation for Economic Cooperation and Development', Centre for Educational Research and Innovation. Also at http://www.learner.org.

—— (1996) *Adult Learning in a New Technological Era*, Paris: OECD Proceedings.

Evans, T. (1995) 'Globalisation, post-Fordism and Open and Distance Education', *Distance Education*, vol. 16, no. 2.

Farmer, E. (1997) 'The Assessment Process with Partners', proceedings of the conference *Cultural Adaptation of Distance Learning*, 28–29 October, Walton Hall: The Open University Business School.

Feller, G. (1995) 'East Meets West – Online', *Internet World*, March, pp. 48–50.

Field, J. (1995) 'Globalisation, Consumption and the Learning Business', *Distance Education*, vol. 16, no. 2.

Financial Times (1996) 5 September, vol. 14, no. 31.

Gayol, Y. (1996) 'The Role of Culture in the Integration of Distance Education: The Mexican Perspective' in M. Thompson (ed.) *Internationalism in Distance Education: A Vision for Higher Education*, ACSDE Research Monograph No. 10, Pennsylvania State University, PA.

Gibson, S. (1996) 'Is All Coherence Gone? The Role of Narrative in Web Design', *IPCT*, vol. 4, no. 2, pp. 7–26.

Gilbert, A. (1996) 'The Virtual University?' in G. Hart and J. Mason (eds) *The Virtual University?*, Symposium Proceedings and Case Studies, University of Melbourne.

Goldberg, M. (1996) 'CALOS: First Results from an Experiment in Computer-Aided Learning', http://homebrew1.cs.ubc.ca/webct/papers/calos.

Goodman, J. (1995) 'Change without Difference: School Restructuring in Historical Perspective', *Harvard Educational Review*, 65, pp. 1–29.

Granger, D. and Gulliver, K. (1996) 'Dynamic Assessment: Quality Assurance in Open and Distance Learning' in M. Thompson (ed.) *Internationalism in Distance Education: A Vision for Higher Education*, ACSDE Research Monograph No. 10, Pennsylvania State University, PA.

Harasim, L, Calvert, T and Groeneboer, C. (1997) 'Virtual-U: A Web-Based System to Support Collaborative Learning' in B. Khan (ed.) *Web-Based Instruction*, New Jersey: Educational Technology Publications.

Harasim, L., Hiltz, S., Teles, L. and Turoff, M. (1995) *Learning Networks*, Cambridge, Mass: MIT Press.

Hiltz, R. (1997) 'Impacts of College-level Courses via Asynchronous Learning Networks: Some Preliminary Results', *JALN*, vol. 1, no. 2, August.

Khan, B. (ed.) (1997) *Web-Based Instruction*, New Jersey: Educational Technology Publications.

Kingsley, J. (1997) 'Trials and Tribulations of an ESL Learner', proceedings of the conference *Cultural Adaptation of Distance Learning*, 28–29 October, Walton Hall: The Open University Business School.

Klemm, W. and Snell, J. (1996) 'Enriching Computer-Mediated Group Learning by Coupling Constructivism with Collaborative Learning', *Journal of Instructional Science and Technology*, vol. 1, no. 2.

Knight, P. (1996) 'Quality in Higher Education and the Assessment of Student Learning', invited address to the EECAE 96.

Latchem, C., Mitchell, J. and Atkinson, R. (1994) 'ISDN-based Videoconferencing in Australian Tertiary Education' in R. Mason and P. Bacsich (eds) *ISDN Application in Education and Training*, London: The Institution of Electrical Engineers.

Le Grew, D. (1995) 'Global Knowledge: Superhighway or Super Gridlock' in *Applications of Media and Technology in Higher Education*, Chiba, Japan: National Institute of Multimedia Education.

Lin, F., Danielson, R. and Herrgott, S. (1996) 'Adaptive Interaction through WWW' in P. Carlson and F. Makedon (eds) *Educational Telecommunications, 1996*, proceedings of ED-TELECOM 96, Association for the Advancement of Computing in Education, Charlottesville, VA.

Lundin, R. (1996) 'International Education 3: Opening Access or Educational Invasion?' paper delivered at the Internationalising Communities Conference, University of Southern Queensland, 29 November.

Macdonald, J. and Mason, R. (1997) 'Information Handling Skills and Resource Based Learning', *Open Learning*, vol. 12, no. 3.

MacFarlane, A. (1992) *Teaching and Learning in an Expanding Higher Education System*, Report of a Working Party of the Committee of Scottish University Principals, Edinburgh: SCFC.

McIntosh, N. and Oliveras, E. (eds) (1996) 'Impact of Information Technology on Higher Education', JHPIEGO, vol. 1, Baltimore: Johns Hopkins University.

McLoughlin, C. (1994) 'An Evaluation of the Technologies and Services of the TAFE Media Network', Perth: Curriculum and Customised Training Network.

McMechan, P. and Matthewson, C. (1994) 'A Commonwealth Asia/Pacific Distance Education Network' in T. Nunan (ed.) *Distance Education Futures*, pp. 207–20, Adelaide: University of South Australia.

Mason, R. (1993) 'The Textuality of Computer Networking' in R. Mason (ed.) *Computer Conferencing: The Last Word*, Victoria, BC: Beach Holme Publishers.

—— (1994a) *Using Communications Media in Open and Flexible Learning*, London: Kogan Page.

—— (1994b) *Evaluation Report on Courses over JANUS – Vol. 1*, Delta Deliverable, Brussels: European Commission.

—— (1995) 'Using Electronic Networking for Assessment' in F. Lockwood (ed.) *Open and Distance Learning Today*, London: Routledge.

—— (1996a) 'Large Scale Distance Teaching and the Convergence of Telecommunications and Multimedia' in C. McBeath and R. Atkinson (eds) *The Learning Superhighway*, proceedings of the Third International Interactive Multimedia Symposium, Perth, January.

—— (1996b) 'Old World Visits New', *Innovations in Education and Training International*, vol. 33, no. 1, pp. 68–9.

Mason, R. and Kaye, A. (eds) (1989) *Mindweave: Communication, Computers and Distance Education*, Oxford: Pergamon.

Moore, M. (1996) 'Is There a Cultural Problem in International Distance Education?' in M. Thompson (ed.) *Internationalism in Distance Education: A Vision for Higher Education*, ACSDE Research Monograph No. 10, Pennsylvania State University, PA.

Morris, T. (1997) 'The Role of Residential Schools', proceedings of the conference *Cultural Adaptation of Distance Learning*, 28–29 October, Walton Hall: The Open University Business School.

Mulholland, P. and Tyler, S. (1997) 'Stadium Events for IBM Students. A Report on Research and Findings So Far', The Open University, Internal Report.

Naidu, S. (1997) 'Collaborative Reflective Practice: A Teaching and Learning Architecture for the Internet', *Distance Education*, vol. 18, no. 2, 257–83.

O'Donnell, J. (1996) 'Teaching on the Infobahn' in D. Corrigan (ed.) *The Internet University. College Courses by Computer*, Harwich, MA: Cape Software Press.

Oliver, R. and Short, G. (1996) 'The Western Australian Telecentres Network: Enhancing Equity and Access to Education in Rural Communities' in P. Carlson and F. Makedon (eds) *Educational Telecommunications, 1996*, proceedings of ED-TELECOM 96, Association for the Advancement of Computing in Education, Charlottesville, VA.

OLS News, June 1995, 'An International WWW Course'.

Open University (1995) 'International Strategy Review', Internal memorandum.

—— (1996) 'Response to the Dearing Review of Higher Education', Internal document.

—— (1996a) Internal document.

—— (1996b) Internal document.

Petre, M., Carswell, L., Price, B. and Thomas, P. (1997) 'Innovations in Large-scale Supported Distance Teaching: Transformation for the Internet, not just Translation', Research Report No. 97/05, Department of Computing, The Open University, Milton Keynes.

Porter, J. (1993) 'Business Re-engineering in Higher Education', *CAUSE/EFFECT*, Winter, pp. 39–46.

Poster, M. (1990) *The Mode of Information. Poststructuralism and Social Context*, Cambridge: Polity Press.

Pritchard, A. (1995) 'The Globalisation of Higher Education', paper presented at the fifth SEAMO INNOTECH International Conference, *Educational Challenges in the World Community of the 21st Century*, Manila: 5–7 December.

Rebelsky, S. (1996) 'Improving WWW-aided Instruction: A report from Experience' in P. Carlson and F. Makedon (eds) *Educational Telecommunications, 1996*, proceedings of ED-TELECOM 96, Association for the Advancement of Computing in Education, Charlottesville, VA.

Reid, K. (1996) 'Student Attitudes Towards Distance Learning' at http://www.att.com/cedl/reabst.html.

Reinhardt, A. (1995) 'New Ways to Learn', *BYTE Magazine*, March.

Robinson, B. (1992) 'Applying Quality Standards in Distance and Open Learning', *EADTU News*, 11, pp. 11–17.

Romiszowski, A. (1997) 'Web-Based Distance Learning and Teaching: Revolutionary Invention or Reaction to Necessity?' in B. Khan (ed.) *Web-Based Instruction*, New Jersey: Educational Technology Publications.

Salmon, G. and Giles, K. (1997) 'Training Virtual Management Tutors', *European Journal of Open and Distance Learning*, June.

Spender, D. (1995) *Nattering on the Net. Women, Power and Cyberspace*, Melbourne: Spinifex.

Stacey, E. and Thompson, L. (1996) 'The Virtual Campus: Deaking University's Experiences' in G. Hart and J. Mason (eds) *The Virtual University?*, Symposium Proceedings and Case Studies, University of Melbourne.

Stapleton, T. (1997) 'An Introduction to the Conference', proceedings of the conference *Cultural Adaptation of Distance Learning*, 28–29 October, Walton Hall: The Open University Business School.

Stoddart, J. (1996) 'Quality Assurance of Overseas Partnerships', Report of the Pilot Audits 1996, Higher Education Quality Council, UK.

Tait, A. (1996) 'From a Domestic to an International Organization: The Open University UK and Europe' in M. Thompson (ed.) *Internationalism in Distance Education: A Vision for Higher Education*, ACSDE Research Monograph No. 10, Pennsylvania State University, PA.

Talbott, S. (1995) *The Future Does Not Compute*, Sebastopol, CA: O'Reilly and Associates.

Taylor, J. and Swannell, P. (1997) 'From Outback to Internet: Crackling Radio to Virtual Campus' in proceedings of *InterAct97*, September, International Telecommunications Union, Geneva.

Taylor, P. (1996) 'Academics' Views' in G. Hart and J. Mason (eds) *The Virtual University?*, Symposium Proceedings and Case Studies, University of Melbourne.

Thach, E. and Murphy, K. (1996) 'Collaboration in Distance Education: From Local to International Perspectives' in M. Thompson (ed.) *Internationalism in Distance Education: A Vision for Higher Education*, ACSDE Research Monograph, No. 10, American Center for the Study of Distance Education, Pennsylvania State University, PA.

Thorne, E. (1997) 'Crossing Cultures: Supporting the Learner in Russia', proceedings of the conference *Cultural Adaptation of Distance Learning*, 28–29 October, Walton Hall: The Open University Business School.

Thorpe, M. (1996) 'Technology and Assessment: Issues for Distance Education', Teaching and Consultancy Centre Report 92, Institute of Educational Technology, The Open University, Milton Keynes.

Trindade, A. (1996) 'Globalization of Distance Education: Setting a Trans-Atlantic

Policy for Collaboration' in M. Thompson (ed.) *Internationalism in Distance Education: A Vision for Higher Education*, ACSDE Research Monograph No. 10, Pennsylvania State University, PA.

Umbriaco, M. and Paquette, D. (1996) 'Courses and Graduate Program Development in DENAID (Distance Education, National and International Development)' in M. Thompson (ed.) *Internationalism in Distance Education: A Vision for Higher Education*, ACSDE Research Monograph No. 10, Pennsylvania State University, PA.

Unsworth, J. (1994) 'Constructing the Virtual Campus', paper delivered to the Modern Language Association Conference, Toronto.

Walsh, B. (1997) 'Three Ws in Nutrition: Two Universities Working Together' in J. Field (ed.) *Electronic Pathways: Adult Learning and the New Communication Technologies*, Leicester: NIACE.

Witherspoon, J. (1997) *Distance Education: A Planner's Casebook*, Boulder, CO: Western Interstate Commission for Higher Education.

Yang, S. (1996) 'Designing Instructional Applications Using Constructive Hypermedia', *Educational Technology*, vol. XXXVI, no. 6, pp. 45–50.

Index